50 *Hikes*

In Coastal and Southern Maine

From the Mahoosuc Range to Mount Desert Island

JOHN GIBSON

Third Edition

Backcountry Guides

Woodstock, Vermont

A Note to the Reader

Every effort is made to provide accurate and up-to-date trail descriptions in this guide. Hazards are noted where known. Users of this volume are reminded that they alone are responsible for their own safety when on the trail, and that they walk the routes described in this guide at their own risk. The author, publisher, and distributors of *50 Hikes in Coastal and Southern Maine* assume no responsibility for any injury, misadventure, or loss occurring from use of the information contained herein.

An Invitation to the Reader

Over time trails can be rerouted and signs and landmarks altered. If you find that changes have occurred on the routes described in this book, please let us know so that corrections may be made in future editions. The author and publisher also welcome other comments and suggestions. Address all correspondence to:

Editor, 50 Hikes™ Series
Backcountry Guides
PO Box 748
Woodstock, VT 05091

Library of Congress Cataloging-in-Publication Data

Gibson, John, 1940–
    50 hikes in coastal and southern Maine : from the Mahoosuc Range to Mount Desert Island / John Gibson.—3rd ed.
        p. cm. – (50 hikes series)
    Rev. ed. of: 50 hikes in southern and coastal Maine. 2nd ed. c1996.
    Includes index.
    ISBN 0-88150-488-2 (alk. paper)
    1. Hiking–Maine–Guidebooks. 2. Maine–Guidebooks. I. Title: Fifty hikes in coastal and southern Maine. II. Gibson, John, 1940– 50 hikes in southern and coastal Maine. III. Title. IV. Fifty hikes series.

GV199.42.M2 G54 2001
917.4104'44–dc21
                                        00-052950

Published by Backcountry Guides
a division of
The Countryman Press,
P.O. Box 748
Woodstock, VT 05091

Distributed by
W.W. Norton & Company, Inc.
500 Fifth Avenue
New York, NY 10110

Text and cover design by Glenn Suokko
Original trial maps by Richard Widhu; new maps by Mapping Specialists., Ltd., Madison, WI
Cover photograph by John Gibson
All photographs are by the author unless otherwise indicated.

Portions of this book originally appeared in *Fifty Hikes in Maine* by John Gibson (1976, 1989) and *Fifty More Hikes in Maine* by Cloe Catlett (1980), both published by Backcountry Guides
Printed in the United States of America

10 9 8 7 6 5 4 3 2 1

DEDICATION

This book is dedicated to all those people who have, on so many occasions, worked to protect the trails and hills of Maine.

50 Hikes at a Glance

HIKE	REGION
1. Mount Agamenticus	Southwestern Maine
2. Sabattus Mountain	Southwestern Maine
3. Mount Cutler	Southwestern Maine
4. Pleasant Mountain	Southwestern Maine
5. Singlepole Ridge	Southwestern Maine
6. Burnt Meadow Mountain	Southwestern Maine
7. Miles Notch–Great Brook Loop	Southwestern Maine
8. Dodge Point Circuit, Damariscotta	South Coast
9. Mount Battie	Camden Hills
10. Cameron Mountain	Camden Hills
11. Maiden Cliff Loop	Camden Hills
12. Mount Megunticook	Camden Hills
13. Bald Rock Mountain	Camden Hills
14. Ragged Mountain	Camden Hills
15. Bald Mountain	Camden Hills
16. Monhegan South Loop	Monhegan Island
17. Monhegan North Loop	Monhegan Island
18. Monument Hill	Central Region and Oxford Hills
19. Mount Philip	Central Region and Oxford Hills
20. Black Mountain	Central Region and Oxford Hills
21. Bald Mountain–Speckled Mountain	Central Region and Oxford Hills
22. Rumford Whitecap	Central Region and Oxford Hills
23. Deer Hill	Evans Notch Region
24. The Conant Trail	Evans Notch Region
25. Stone House–White Cairn Loop	Evans Notch Region

DISTANCE (in miles)	RISE (in feet)	VIEWS	GOOD FOR KIDS	NOTES
1	350	★	★	Tower, built summit, near town
1	500	★	★	Open views from high ledges
2.5	1,000	★	★	Southerly views, wooded ridge
3.5	1,500	★		Open, grassy summit, tower
3	700	★	★	Winding road, wooded summit
2.5	1,100	★	★	Southern view, wooded summit
11	2,150	★		Long backcountry ridgewalk
2.5	230	★	★	Fine woods and shore walk
1	600	★	★	Short hike to big ocean views
6.3	700	★		Long, easy, wooded loop
2.25	700	★	★	Bold cliffs, water views to west
5.25	1,190	★		Long, interesting ridgewalk
3.5	800	★	★	Woods road, open ocean views
3	850	★	★	Wooded trail, fine ocean views
2	650	★	★	Quiet, easy, inland views
2	50	★	★	Boat trip to lovely island paths
1.75	100	★	★	Boat trip to lovely island paths
1.5	300	★	★	Short, easy loop with views
1	300	★	★	Short point-to point, wooded
3.5	1,250	★		Obscure trail, isolated, views
4	1,500	★		Two summits, grand views
4	1,550	★	★	High, open ridgewalk, ledges
4	1,250	★	★	Wooded loop, spring, ledges
5.5	1,200	★		Superb, remote loop, farmsite
4.25	1,400	★	★	Excellent views from ledges

50 Hikes at a Glance

HIKE	REGION
26. Ames and Speckled Mountains	Evans Notch Region
27. East Royce Mountain	Evans Notch Region
28. Haystack Notch	Evans Notch Region
29. Caribou Mountain	Evans Notch Region
30. The Roost	Evans Notch Region
31. Wheeler Brook	Evans Notch Region
32. Albany Mountain	Evans Notch Region
33. Mount Carlo–Goose Eye Loop	The Mahoosucs
34. Mahoosuc Notch, Speck Pond Loop	The Mahoosucs
35. Old Speck	Grafton Notch
36. Baldpate Mountain	Grafton Notch
37. Pemetic Mountain	Mount Desert Island/Acadia National Park
38. Parkman Mountain and Bald Peak	Mount Desert Island/Acadia National Park
39. Gorham and Champlain Mountains	Mount Desert Island/Acadia National Park
40. Penobscot and Sargent Mountain	Mount Desert Island/Acadia National Park
41. Norumbega Mountain	Mount Desert Island/Acadia National Park
42. Acadia Mountain Loop	Mount Desert Island/Acadia National Park
43. Cadillac Mountain	Mount Desert Island/Acadia National Park
44. Sand Beach and Great Head	Mount Desert Island/Acadia National Park
45. The Bubbles	Mount Desert Island/Acadia National Park
46. St. Sauveur–Flying Mountain Loop	Mount Desert Island/Acadia National Park
47. Beech Mountain	Mount Desert Island/Acadia National Park
48. Great Pond Mountain	Eastern Maine
49. Peaked Mountain (Chick Hill)	Eastern Maine
50. Cutler Coastal Trail Circuit	Eastern Maine

DISTANCE (in miles)	RISE (in feet)	VIEWS	GOOD FOR KIDS	NOTES
8.25	2,150	★		Long, wooded walk, falls
3	1,700	★	★	Short, steep, falls, outlooks
10.5	1,600	★		End-to-end walk and return
7	1,900	★		Remote loop, shelter, falls
1	400	★	★	Short, wooded, river views
9	1,700			Long, wooded, remote loop
4	1,100	★	★	Remote, wooded, moderate
7.25	2,200	★		Superb, isolated ridgeline
11	2,300	★		Remote, tough, difficult path
7.75	2,730	★		Steep, demanding trail, falls
8.5	2,700	★		Long, demanding hike
2.5	950	★	★	Easy, pretty trail to ledges
2.5	700	★	★	Open, ledgy summits, views
6	1,200	★		Fine ridgeline, ocean views
5	1,150	★		Ladders, ledge, sea views
2.75	600	★	★	Ledgy, ocean views, easy
2.5	500	★	★	Spectacular ocean views
7	1,230	★	★	Splendid ocean outlooks
2	200	★	★	Fine strand, ocean views
3.5	800	★	★	Ledgy, open summits
6	1,100	★	★	Fine loop on Somes Sound
3.5	700	★	★	Wooded, quiet, easy walk
4.25	650	★	★	Great, open summit ledges
2.5	800	★	★	Ledgy, open summits, views
5.5	400	★		Oceanside cliff walk, woods

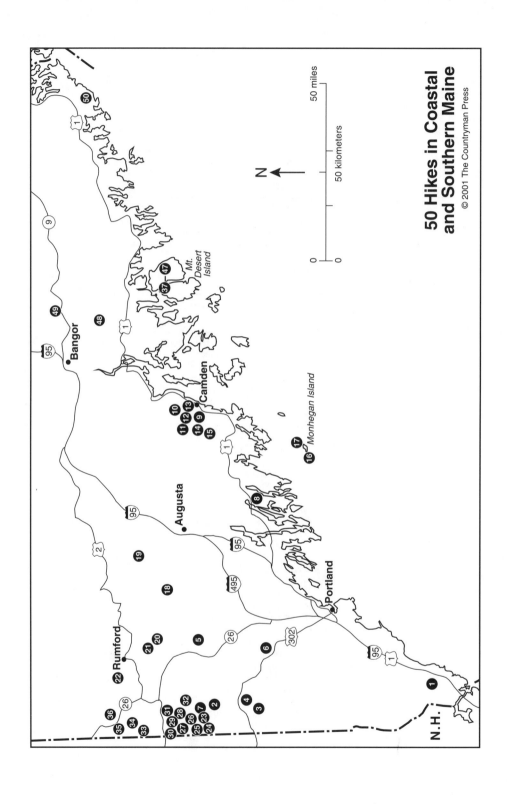

50 Hikes in Coastal and Southern Maine

© 2001 The Countryman Press

Contents

Introduction

Welcome to the reader. I hope you find the walks in this volume to be interesting and challenging. *50 Hikes in Coastal and Southern Maine* (and its predecessor *50 Hikes in Maine*) has celebrated its 25th year in print. Still, this is not an "old" book. I have recently rehiked all the trails described here, and have revised trail directions where necessary. This edition also contains two new hikes—Ragged Mountain and Bald Mountain. You will find a great variety of hiking in these pages, from short, coastal walks suitable for families to major hikes in Maine's mountain regions.

50 Hikes in Coastal and Southern Maine covers all of the Maine coast region and all of Maine south and west of Bangor. From the Cutler Coastal Trail along the wild Atlantic coast of Washington County to the gentle slopes of York County's Mount Agamenticus in the south, this volume will introduce you to some of the best hiking in the Pine Tree State. Hikes are organized into regions, including the South Coast and the Camden Hills, the Central Region and Oxford Hills, Eastern Maine, the Evans Notch Region, Mount Desert Island, and Southwestern Maine. You will even find a section describing walks on fabled Monhegan Island.

For each hike included here, directions for travel and parking have been provided. A topographical map accompanies each hike, as well as information on mileage and altitude gain. Even if you are a novice hiker, you will find this book easy to use and directions easy to follow. As you travel to different trail locations you may find my companion volume *Maine's Most Scenic Roads* (DownEast Books) helpful.

Hiking is as good as ever in Maine, but it will require the active involvement and careful monitoring of everyone who enjoys Maine trails to keep it that way. That means if you use and enjoy the out of doors in Maine, you must do your part. Stay informed of land-use decisions by state and local authorities. Attend hearings when large landholders seek to convert trail lands into clear-cuts or developments. Testify at legislative hearings. Alert your representatives to unsound forestry practices. Join the trail and conservation organizations that are listed at the end of this introduction. Better still, become active in defending Maine's trails and woodlands by participating in the programs of conservation organizations that interest you and by offering them your time and financial support.

It is a privilege to be able to leave the noise and confusion of urban life behind and to walk quiet trails in unspoiled woodlands. The opportunity for such experiences exists because of the countless people who have dedicated themselves to wildlands preservation. Credit for this preservation must go to individual landowners who have kept their land in its natural state, and to environmental and conservation organizations that have fought development and sought to protect streams and rivers. Trail organizations such as the Maine Chapter of the Sierra Club, the Appalachian Mountain Club, and the Maine Appalachian Trail Club have done their part. Government programs, too, such as Land for Maine's Future, have held the line in protecting wildlands. Ultimately, whatever is good about the Maine countryside is a result of the efforts of individuals, people like yourself, who

Pemaquid Point Light

were unwilling to sell their birthright for a mess of potage, and don't want to see Maine lose its essential character.

In recent years, the Maine backcountry has been assaulted by twentieth-century demands for development, "improvement," and subdivision. Condominium developments and vacation home communities climb mountainsides, destroying vegetation and groundcover in many areas of the state. Shoreline and marshland encroach- ment continue to be serious problems. The giant paper companies, most of which are owned by multinationals with offices thou- sands of miles away, have placed vast tracts of Maine land up for sale. In some instances, portions of these tracts have been purchased and held as conservation lands. Far more acreage, however, has been shuffled among those anxious for maximum exploitation of their holdings, regardless of its impact on the Maine landscape.

Forestry practices have deteriorated, and the use of skidders, feller-bunchers, and other engines of destructive industrial forestry have come to dominate. Though controlled by state regulations, clear-cutting is still practiced. Some of Maine's largest timber landholders are regularly cutting at a non-sustainable rate. All of these factors have challenged the stable, quiet, and undisturbed quality of the Maine woods. Land sales and the increased mechanization of forestry in Maine also have shifted the burden of owning such equipment and employing it to smaller cutters who work on a job-contract basis, and who must work under a bid system that forces them to cut faster and with less discrimination than ever before in order to earn a profit. Such cutting practices, when finished, leave the landscape bare, rutted, scarred, and burdened with highly flammable slash.

For many decades, forestry was practiced in a responsible way in Maine, with emphasis on sustainable yields. This is no longer the case. There is a need for vigilance now from all those who believe the woods should be used responsibly and trails kept open in well-managed lands for the use of future generations. This approach will guarantee not only access to a healthy backcountry, but the availability of forest industry jobs, quality forest products, and healthy earnings far into the future.

Trails

The trails described in *50 Hikes in Coastal and Southern Maine* range from easy, well-defined paths along tote roads to demanding, tough-to-follow routes over rock faces, streambeds, and through brushy, rough terrain. The maps and descriptions in this book make finding your way easy, and the trail commentary warns of any noticeable problems along the way. Each hike description was revised and current at press time in 2001, but weathering, blowdowns, and trail relocation may change the direction of a given route at any time. Most trails are "blazed" with paint markers, but some have not been marked recently, or their blazes have weathered bare. Always carry a compass when you are hiking anywhere in Maine, even in settled areas. United States Geological Survey (USGS) and other maps are useful, although not essential, supplements to the maps in this book. (See "Directions and Maps" on page 17.) Beware of Maine's unpredictable climate. Should inclement weather overtake you on the higher peaks, don't continue upward, but always *head down* for safety.

Clothing and Boots

Hiking clothing has always been a matter of personal taste. Major design improvements have made hiking wear a lot more comfortable and functional in the last several years.

Basically, shorts and cotton-synthetic shirts are suitable outerwear for summer. Long pants and a wool shirt, sweater, and wind shell are appropriate for cooler weather. For day hikes, a lightweight poncho or rain jacket of coated nylon or Gore-Tex, a hat, a down vest, and an extra pair of socks are all worthy items for your pack. Carry gloves in spring and fall.

Always overestimate your clothing needs. Temperatures on higher summits are frequently much cooler than those at the roadside. Windchill can leave you cold and shivering even on sunny days when the temperature would normally be comfortable. Prepare accordingly.

Footwear, like clothing, remains a matter of individual preference. Any time a bunch of hikers get together, heated discussions of what is "best" for your feet will likely follow. Maine trails are usually rough, and sneakers and street shoes are out of the question. Vibram-soled boots are preferable, with sturdy, 6-inch uppers. There are many good brands on the market, but they are no longer cheap. A good pair of hiking boots costs from $125 to $200. There are no inexpensive alternatives, for bargain basement boots tend to fall apart on the trail, possibly failing you at a dangerous moment. Jogging shoes and the new boots made with synthetic cloth uppers should be avoided. A quality leather hiking boot will last many years, so we're talking about an investment of only a few dollars for each season's use. Not bad, when you think of it that way.

Low prices may be tempting, but you will do much better if you purchase hiking clothing and boots from an established outdoor or mountaineering store. They will carry the best lines of goods and will be there later if you need assistance. Clothing or boots bought in discount houses are usually second-rate, and the staff know nothing of the sport. As has been said, "You get what you pay for."

Backpacks and Tents

Backpacks have undergone major changes recently. Hikers are getting away from the enormous, unwieldy frame packs that were sold everywhere in the 1980s. Back-hugging soft packs, which carry well and move with you, are now widely available. A good small- to medium-sized rucksack is all you'll need for most day trips in Maine. Larger backpacks for overnighters and extended trips are made by Kelty, Karrimor, North Face, L. L. Bean, REI, Lowe, and Camp Trails. Large frame packs are a poor choice for the Maine backcountry because they tend to catch on every low-hanging branch and bush you pass.

A tent is worth its weight in reliable shelter for longer trips in the Maine mountains. The heavy canvas tentage of 10 years ago

has been replaced by super lightweight portable shelters weighing only 4 or 5 pounds. Sleeping bags are also lighter and more compact. If you choose your equipment carefully, you should be able to get away for several days in the mountains with no more than 30 pounds on your back.

The hikes in this volume are essentially day trips, some of them shorter, some long and demanding. As noted earlier, except for self-designed overnighters, a large day pack or small rucksack should be adequate for the routes described in this book. A larger pack is useful, of course, if you are hiking in the cold-weather seasons, when you will need room to carry extra clothing.

For those who *love* to carry a bigger pack, several routes covered here afford enough distance and remoteness to make splitting the hike into an overnighter feasible. Those hikes that lend themselves to overnighting and that will require a larger pack if you decide to bring along a tent and sleeping bag include: Hike 7–Miles Notch–Great Brook Loop; Hike 24–Conant Trail; Hike 28–Haystack Notch; Hike 29–Caribou Mountain (summit shelter); Hike 31–Wheeler Brook (Hastings Campground lies midroute); Hike 33–Mount Carlo–Goose Eye Loop (shelter); Hike 34–Mahoosuc Notch and Speck Pond Loop (pondside tent platforms); Hike 36–Baldpate Mountain (shelter); and Hike 50–Cutler Coastal Trail.

Cooking

If you're hiking for more than a day or simply want the means to brew up some hot tea or soup, carry your own stove. Chopping down trees and destroying vegetation to build a campfire is not only foolish, it's often illegal as well. There are many excellent backpacking stoves, tiny and lightweight, that operate on white gasoline or butane. Plan meals that lend themselves to one-pot preparation. Your mountaineering shop has freeze-dried foods to supplement the quick meals available in the supermarket.

Drinking Water

Stream pollution is still rare in Maine, but especially near settled areas, it's wise to boil or disinfect your water—or carry in your own safe water. Streams flowing in fields where there are cattle are particularly suspect. Much has been written in the way of warnings about *Giardia* recently. These are naturally occurring parasites, frequently transmitted by beavers, as well as humans, that may occasionally be found in mountain streams and ponds. They cause a most unpleasant affliction, as the parasitic cysts fasten themselves to the stomach lining and cause nausea, cramps, diarrhea, and transient feverish symptoms. It would, however, take an awful lot of heavily infested water passing through your body to create the likelihood of a really bad case of giardiasis. Still, it's wisest to get your water from a reliable spring, or if you must use stream water, choose a fast-moving stream and then boil, disinfect, or filter it. Better still, fill your water bottle back home or at a known safe water site whenever possible.

Hiking with Children

Hiking is a great experience for children and an excellent family activity. The pastime can foster in children an appreciation of the woods and conservation that will endure for a lifetime. Hiking too far with children *who are too young* is a different story. Most of the trails in this book can be navigated by children who are at least 6 or 7 years of age. Where terrain is difficult or severe, the text so indicates, and such trails are probably not good family choices to pursue with youngsters.

Kids don't have the endurance of adults, and little legs have to work harder on the trail, so plenty of thought should be given to distance as well as elevation. Attempting hikes of 4 or more miles with children who are only 4 or 5 years old usually is much too taxing and will result in a spoiled trip for everyone, with tired, cranky youngsters who have to be carried a good part of the way. Parents should use sound judgment in carefully estimating the hiking ability of their youngsters and not push young children into long, forced marches beyond their ability. The purpose of being in the woods is for all, young and old, to enjoy themselves, right?

Involving kids in plant, tree, and landmark identification can boost their enjoyment of any hike. Informal instruction in the use of a compass and map reading will also help them trace their route and prepare them for safe hiking later on their own. A backpack well stocked with interesting snacks and beverages will help combat the fatigue factor, too.

Directions and Maps

For easy reference, always carry this book or a photocopy of the hike as you walk so that both trail description and map are readily available. Each hike description lists the total distance you will walk from start to finish, from roadside to summit and return. Approximate vertical rise is also listed, giving you some idea of the *total* amount of climbing you'll be doing, as some trails rise and descend several times before the greatest elevation is reached. The suggested hiking time for each route is based on comfortable walking time, not a mad dash. There are many summits on which you'll want to linger, enjoying the view and the Maine air.

The maps in this book have been prepared on backgrounds taken from US Geological Survey (USGS) maps. The hikes described

On the Bald Rock Mountain Trail (see Hike 13)

were drawn in, together with important trail-side features (see the key at the end of the introduction), after the text had been pre-pared and thus reflect trail routes and the latest information available at the time of pub-lication. The use of USGS maps as back-ground is designed to show contours and generally give the hiker a feel for the land he or she will be hiking.

You will not need maps other than those in this book to make the hikes, but at the begin-ning of each hike I have listed maps that can provide additional information on geographi-cal features—and on the views you will see from the mountaintops. Most of those listed are USGS maps, which can be obtained at many book, sports, and hardware stores throughout Maine, or directly from the USGS. For those hikes using sections of the Appala-chian Trail, the maps published by the Maine Appalachian Trail Club (MATC) are also use-ful. In addition, the Appalachian Mountain Club's maps cover sections of the Mahoosuc Range in Maine, the Rangeley region, Acadia National Park, some of the Camden Hills, and Baxter State Park. For ordering addresses, see the end of this section.

A word of caution is in order regarding USGS maps. For a few Maine areas, the older, less detailed 15-minute series may be all you can find. Maps in that series, made as far back as the 1930s in some cases, may be seriously out of date. To-pography is, of course, unchanged, but long-vanished houses, fire towers, roads, railroad tracks, and trails may still be shown, while new roads and trails do not appear. Remapping has continued, however, and the more useful 7½-minute USGS series is now available for most of the state. You should insist on the new series if you buy additional USGS maps at a store.

Resources

For further information about hiking opportunities in Maine and the conservation of Maine's wilderness, you may wish to write or to call one or more of the following organizations:

US Geological Survey
Branch of Information Services
Box 25286, Denver Federal Center
Denver, CO 80225
303-202-4700

Maine Appalachian Trail Club
Box 283
Augusta, ME 04330

Appalachian Mountain Club
5 Joy Street
Boston, MA 02108
617-523-0636
www.outdoors.org

Maine Audubon Society
188 US Route 1
Falmouth, ME 04105
207-781-2330
www.maineaudubon.org

RESTORE: The North Woods
9 Union Street
Hallowell, ME 04347
www.restore.org

New England Sierra Club
5 Joy Street
Boston, MA 02108
www.sierraclub.org

Maine Coast Heritage Trust
167 Park Row
Brunswick, ME 04011
207-729-7366

Natural Resources Council of Maine
271 State Street
Augusta, ME 04330
207-622-3101

The Nature Conservancy
Box 338
122 Main Street
Topsham, ME 04086
207-729-5181
www.tnc.org

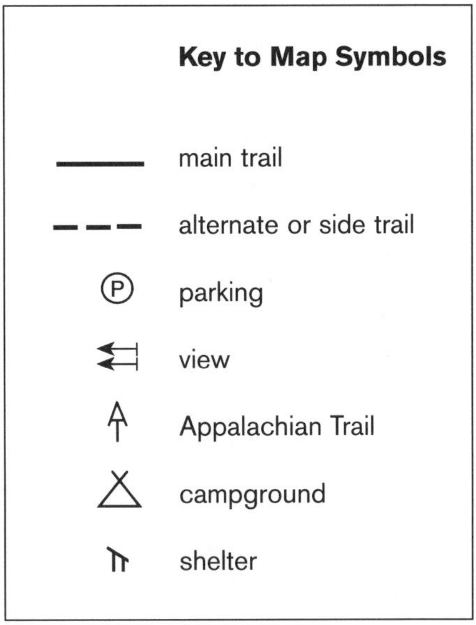

Key to Map Symbols

——— main trail

— — — alternate or side trail

Ⓟ parking

view

Appalachian Trail

campground

shelter

I

Southwestern Maine

1

Mount Agamenticus

Distance (round trip): 1 mile

Hiking time: 50 minutes

Vertical rise: 350 feet

Map: USGS 7½' York Harbor

Mount Agamenticus, in exchange for an easy, brief hike, offers superb views. It is no more than a ledgy hummock on the coastal map that you can scramble up in short order, but the perspective from the summit belies its elevation. A good destination for some light afternoon tramping in spring and autumn, Agamenticus is easily accessible from Boston and Portland.

The mountain can be reached either from the Maine Turnpike (I-95) or from US 1 in the Cape Neddick section of York. If you travel via I-95, take the York exit and cross to the west side of the highway. Turn right or north on Chase's Pond Road, which parallels the interstate. Follow this route approximately 3 miles northward to a junction with Mountain Road, on which you continue in a more westerly direction. If you approach the mountain from US 1, turn west in Cape Neddick on Mountain Road (sometimes called Agamenticus Road) and drive westward, intersecting Chase's Pond Road in 1.3 miles. From this junction, drive west another 2.7 miles, where the paved road ends abruptly. Park your car here at the foot of the summit road.

The path to the summit departs through the trees on an old woods road by the gravel parking area. The way leads gradually upward through tall pines and fir, coming shortly to a junction. Keep left here, rising more briskly through denser growth and to the northwest through a crumbling stone wall. The path soon emerges in a clearing just to the right side of the mountain road where the power line crosses. Keep to the right and under the power line

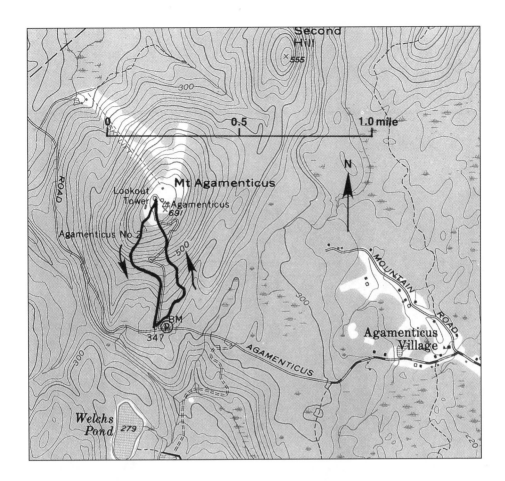

as it climbs northward and away from the road up a series of granite ledges. Unmarked here, the route is easily followed over the rock. Thin stands of red oak, yellow pine, and scattered, immature birch line both sides of the corridor.

Climbing steadily, the way shortly crosses the road (watch for speeding cars) and continues up through a gully bordered by scrub oak. Just below the summit road, the path bends slightly to the left, crosses a grassy spot, and emerges on the left side of the road opposite a telephone relay tower. Follow the road straight to the fire tower and to the left of the main summit

buildings, which are not open to the public.

Agamenticus's summit bears the fallen-down remains of a ski operation. Rusty stanchions, once active in pulling skiers up the north side of the mountain, stand alone, looking like lost, old men. No matter; climb the lookout tower and enjoy the fine, 360-degree view. If the tower observer is in during summer, you might be invited to climb into the cabin and share the perspective, the forest service radio crackling in the background.

To the north-northwest are the low hills of Sanford and Ossipee Hill in Waterboro. On exceptionally fine days (some of the

Looking north from the summit of Mount Agamenticus

best of which come in winter), you may be able to see Mount Washington and other peaks in New Hampshire's Presidential Range. York village lies southeast of your lookout, with Kittery and Portsmouth farther down the coast and more around to the south. East and northeast, you'll have excellent views up the southern Maine coast and, of course, out toward the Atlantic. A fair variety of bird life may be seen from the tower and in the woods around the summit. One afternoon, I spent nearly an hour watching a turkey vulture ride the thermals, looking for dinner, about a half mile to the west.

To head down, go back to the point where you emerged onto the road by the telephone relay disks, and turn right, entering the woods farther west by a bent tree. Here, the path drops slowly to the southwest and south through evergreens and mixed growth. The grade becomes steeper and, in about ¼ mile, you come to a T with an old tote road. Bear left here, walking south and east, and you'll soon emerge on the paved mountain road. Simply follow it down to the base.

For an introduction to Agamenticus' tower and many other fire towers in Maine, living or gone, read *From York to the*

Allagash, Forest Fire Lookouts in Maine (Moosehead Communications, Greenville, Maine) by sometime Agamenticus tower-man David N. Hilton. The terrain on Agamenticus has been partially logged in recent years and some alteration made to structures and grounds on the summit. Additions to preserved lands around the mountain are anticipated. Ongoing changes of this type may affect trail location and routing. Check locally for alterations in the route described here.

2

Sabattus Mountain

Distance (round trip): 1 mile

Hiking time: 40 minutes

Vertical rise: 500 feet

Map: USGS 7½' North Waterford

Good things sometimes come in small packages—and that goes for mountains, too. Sabattus (elevation 1,280 feet) is short work, but it offers one of the finest mountain panoramas I know. And you needn't go all that far north in the Pine Tree State to enjoy the view.

Getting to the trailhead is simple. From the intersection of ME 5 and ME 5A in Center Lovell, head north on ME 5, turning right onto a paved road after 0.7 mile. At 1.5 miles from ME 5, a gravel road forks right, uphill. Turn here, and proceed about 0.3 mile to a parking area on your left, just past the Willoby place.

The trail leaves opposite the parking area and is marked by a weathered sign next to a great old pine. Walk west and southwest through dense, tall pines, beech, and an occasional maple. You'll quickly reach a fine, mossy stone wall; turn sharply toward the south, walking parallel to the old wall.

At ½ mile, you leave the evergreen groves, cross another stone wall, and head south and southeast through young second-growth hardwoods. Shortly, ascend steeply out of this cut-over area, heading up the lower peak.

The trail levels off momentarily, then recommences climbing to a broad, ledgy area topped by a stark, weathered pine. Continue over this rise, through a slump, and climb directly to the main summit, the former site of the now dismantled fire tower.

The great cliffs that form the southwest flanks of Sabattus are immediately below

South from Sabattus Mountain

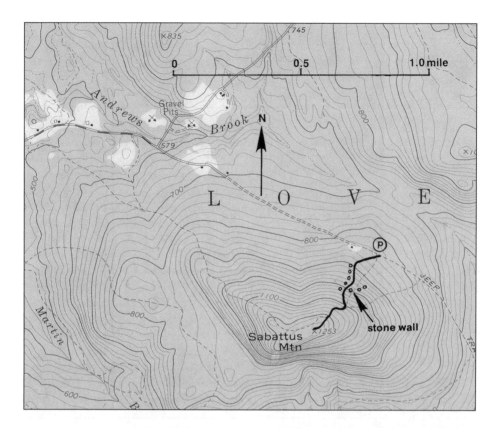

you. The views range splendidly from southeast to northwest. The imposing mass of Pleasant Mountain in Bridgton is nearly due south over Kezar Pond. More to your right, you can see into North Conway, where the drumlin-shaped mass that holds Cathedral and White Horse ledges is visible. To the west, beyond Kezar Lake, stretch the Presidentials, Robbins Ridge above Kearsarge, and the Carter-Moriah Range. Sharply northwest are the mountains below and around Evans Notch. It's truly a fine sight; this is a perch you'll not quickly abandon. Eminently worth some camera work on a clear day before you make the quick descent to your car.

3

Mount Cutler

Distance (round trip): 2½ miles

Hiking time: 2 hours

Vertical rise: 1,000 feet

Map: USGS 7½' Cornish and Hiram

West of Sebago and looming over the banks of the Saco River, Mount Cutler in Hiram offers fine day hiking in a quiet corner of western Maine not far from the New Hampshire state line. This hogback provides some really excellent views for a relatively low mountain, and you take in the whole panorama of New Hampshire's White Mountains on this ridge walk. Hiram is a quiet, country crossroads, and it escapes the summer bustle of those towns eastward around Sebago. A visit to the village and the mountain offers an unhurried experience in a very attractive region of the Pine Tree State.

To reach the mountain, drive to the junction of ME 117 and ME 5 in Hiram, where a modern bridge spans the Saco. On the west side of the bridge, go south on a local road to the village store, bearing immediately right on Mountain View Road. Just around the bend you'll find parking by some abandoned railroad tracks to the right of the road.

The trail lies to the left of and across the tracks from the parking area. You head immediately uphill to a grove of towering white pines. Shortly, bear *right* at a junction and proceed southwest on a tote road. Cresting the rise, this road ends at a small basin on your left, bordered by beeches. Big buttresses of rock and ledge are before you, and it's up these exposed granite arms that the trail proceeds.

Passing the basin and the small, seasonal stream that drains it, head west and southwest as the trail quickly ascends. Zigzag over a series of ledges and follow the left bank of another seasonal brook upward into a ravine. In ⅛ mile, you *cross* this brook to your right by

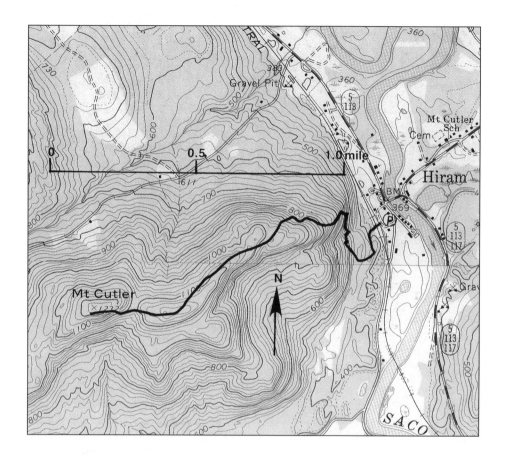

a large boulder in a tangle of blowdown. (Don't continue upward, to the left, on the apparent path of a little-used trail.) You now scramble up a steep dirt track, turning gradually northward, passing directly under some ledgy overhangs. This route is erratically marked by red-orange paint blazes on trees. You must scout them carefully or you'll miss them and the turn just described.

The trail now slabs the lip of exposed rock as you walk northwest. Trail blazes are sometimes hard to spot, but the path is obvious as it hugs the edge of the hillside. Views over Hiram and the Saco begin to open up. You come soon to a more level spot in a grove of oaks. In winter, the trees are bare and good views northward toward

the Presidential Range may be seen here.

You next turn sharply left (southwest) under the oaks and move quickly upward again in scattered young balsams and Norway spruce. Pass through several small clearings as the trail pulls around to the west, ascending more gradually over grassy ledge. In a few minutes, turn left onto open ledge with spectacular outlooks over the Saco River valley to the east, south, and southwest. This spot makes an excellent lunch site or rest stop before you move on. Douglas Hill lies eastward. The hills above Cornish form a ridge to the south. Heading generally southeastward, the meandering Saco bisects the pretty valley on its way toward the Atlantic.

The view from Mount Cutler's summit

To continue, follow the trail west and southwest as it winds through mixed growth along the spine of the hogback. Occasional open places provide an opportunity to gaze at the Presidential Range to the northwest. The massive, elongated summit in the foreground is Pleasant Mountain in Bridgton. The east summit of Cutler is reached about ¾ mile above the road, and, as the trail pulls around in an arc toward the southwest, you reach the main summit 1 ⅓ miles from where you parked. From the first height-of-land to Cutler's main peak, you cross open grassy ledges that are thinly wooded, offering more good views of the valley. Cutler isn't a high mountain, but this combination of light forestation and exposed ledge makes for striking, panoramic views that compete favorably with those of much higher peaks. The return to your car is made by retracing your route. Use care while descending.

The round trip to the main summit can be done in less than 2 hours, but it is wise to allow for a more leisurely pace. Unless you're used to such things, the initial steep scramble up to the ledges will slow you down, and it's prudent to allow extra time for this section, particularly if you hike Mount Cutler when snow and ice are present. Use extra caution if descending on ice.

4

Pleasant Mountain

Distance (round trip): 3½ miles

Hiking time: 3 hours

Vertical rise: 1,500 feet

Map: USGS 7½' Pleasant Mountain

Pleasant Mountain is an impressive, rangy mountain that rises dramatically west of Moose Pond in Bridgton and Denmark. The north end of the mountain contains a ski area, but the rest of this big peak remains forested and unspoiled.

On US 302, drive about 4 miles north and west from the center of Bridgton to the road that serves the ski area on the mountain's northeast slope. Take this road (the first left off US 302 after you pass Moose Pond) and watch for trail signs just over 3 miles south of US 302. A new parking shoulder has been built on the east side of the road. Make sure your car is fully off the road and not blocking traffic when you park.

The Ledges Trail, sometimes called the Moose Trail, begins its ascent from the east side of the mountain along the route of a gravel fire road. Paint blazes mark the route for its entire length. You walk first northwest and west up the broad fire road, passing through patches of wild raspberries. Shortly the road narrows to a trail eroded by water. Climbing steadily west and southwest, you reach a fork in the road (which is again wider at this point). Bear left here, and—as you make an easy arc more toward the southwest—cross two small brooks in an area thickly grown up with young birch, beech, and cherry.

You then begin the steeper climb up to the ledges as you wind west up the ridge. The trail in this section suffered a lot of damage from winter blowdowns in an ice storm in early 1998, and there still may be short sections that go around blocked areas. At just under 1 mile, you climb over

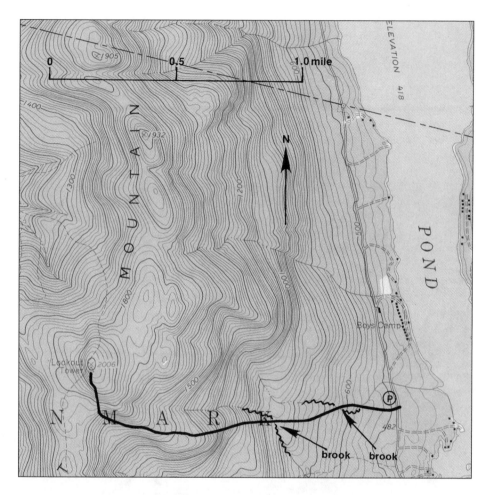

outcrops of Chatham granite that indicate the beginning of the ledges. Soon you move up out of the trees and merge onto the ledges proper.

There are fine views here to the southwest, south, and to the southeast over Moose Pond. Continue by climbing gradually around to the northwest, with the southwest hump of the mountain becoming visible through the young oaks along the trail.

You soon pass over a second open ledge area with good views to the west and southwest. Meandering first northeast and then northwest again, you climb more

steeply over ground covered with low-bush blueberries, scramble over more ledge, and pass a third open ledge, which looks to the west. Turn northeast again, climb over an outcrop, and then turn north. In a few yards you'll reach the summit and fire tower on a grassy lawn that was once the site of the Pleasant Mountain House.

The views to the west and northwest from the "Green Pinnacle" are spectacular on a clear day. The Presidentials in New Hampshire stretch north to south on the distant horizon. Carter Dome is clearly visible over the west tongue of Pleasant. Tiny

Views to the southwest from the summit of Pleasant Mountain

Kezar Pond and the narrow thread of Kezar Lake lie to the northwest, while Lovell Pond near Fryeburg can be seen to the southwest. The fire tower, abandoned by the State of Maine, is not staffed, and the ladder has been partially removed. To descend, retrace your steps for a brisk downward hike of about 50 minutes.

5

Singlepole Ridge (Singepole Mountain)

Distance (round trip): 3 miles

Hiking time: 2 hours

Vertical rise: 700 feet

Maps: USGS 7½' Oxford; USGS 15' Poland

Tucked in rolling countryside between Buckfield and South Paris, Singlepole Ridge (or Singepole Mountain, as locals call it) provides some undemanding but interesting walking through pretty back-country to a rangy, open summit with fine views over a wide area. In the heart of Oxford County, Singlepole is accessible via easy grades on woods roads that can be managed by children over 5, and the mountain is thus a favorite walk for family outings and even cross-country skiing or snowshoeing, in season.

Singlepole is approached via ME 117 from South Paris or Buckfield. Turn south onto a side road off 117 just over 2 miles east of its junction with ME 119 in South Paris, or 7.5 miles west of 117's junction with ME 140 in Buckfield. Follow this side road (clearly marked BRETT HILL ROAD) uphill past a farmhouse for just over 0.4 mile. Where the paved road bears sharply right and a gravel road continues straight ahead, park your car off the road in a sandy area to your left.

Begin the walk by following the gravel road south, climbing steadily in the direction of the ridge. Though unmarked, this gravel right-of-way is known as Durrell Hill Road, named for the first rise that you are ascending. Cars do make it up in here, but you'll see by the occasional deep ruts and washouts why this section is more happily navigated on foot. Your route rises steadily through attractive mixed cover for another ⁴/₁₀ mile, where you arrive at a clearing and road junction. Durrell Hill Road now continues due south up the elevation of that

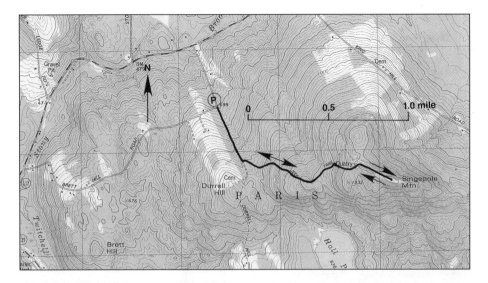

name, but you bear *left* (east) by an elabo-rate old cellar hole marked by crumbling foundation stones. The cellar hole has been taken over by black oak, beech, and birch saplings.

The trail next follows a rough tote road east and southeast toward Singlepole Ridge. Nowhere is this trail marked with blazes, but you can easily find your way if you stick to the main track. White pine, more black oak, birch, and scrub charac-terize the woods here, which densely crowd the road. Scattered balsam intrudes, as do clumps of silver glade fern. The right-of-way begins soon to show the signs of weathering and resembles less a road than a kind of dished channel. Bars of exposed ledge show themselves, and several brushy tote roads appear on both your left and your right.

You shortly come to a point where the road pulls to your right, but you can see another route in front of you up a washed-out series of ledgy bars. Continue south and southeast up these rocks and at the top reconnect with the road, which runs eastward once more. Passing groves of

young hemlock, the track leads through an open area grown up in white birch, black birch, and maple. A ground cover of low-bush blueberries borders the road. Head-ing south-southeast, you crest a rise and enter a broad clearing in a few more minutes.

Birds and small animals abound on this wooded hillside. I have seen coyote scat, deer signs, and the tracks of partridge and rabbit. A wide variety of seasonal birds and some that are here all year–such as the black-capped chickadee–may be visible. Although I have not noticed their tracks, this is the type of dense cover favored, too, by black bear.

Beyond the clearing you continue east-ward through several low spots, and the route pulls south and then east again, com-ing soon to an open area where there is a grassy passing place. Ahead of you there are three roads. To your left, barely visible, is a brushy, grown-up track that heads to the site of some old mining operations. To your right is a gravel track that pulls to the south. Stay on the wider, *middle* track and continue southeastward.

Summit Ledges, Singlepole Ridge

Keeping left at another junction and running eastward, the trail rises through more climax forest and then pulls around to the south again for the final rise to a large, open clearing underlain by pegmatitic granite. Walk past a small, flooded quarry hole and continue uphill to the south. Some good outlooks on the western Maine hills and White Mountains of New Hampshire begin to open up on your right. Birds move quickly around this open space, and birds of prey are in evidence. I have seen an American kestrel hunting these stony plains and have watched an impressive northern goshawk lazily circling the main summit.

Continuing southeastward, pass through some tall spruce and stay with the track as it dips slightly, passes a path that runs west, and rises through more trees to emerge on the elongated, ledgy main summit. Although bordered by trees, there are openings here with excellent views in all directions. Views to the northwest reveal the major peaks in the Rangeley region. To the east are the fine, rolling hills of central Maine, and, most obviously, the ledgy, granitic flanks of Streaked Mountain. Over to the southwest you will see both Hall Pond and, farther off, Thompson Lake. The long, humpy summit in the middle distance to the west is Pleasant Mountain (Hike 4).

The great bubble of pegmatitic granite that underlies this ridge is evident as you stroll around the pleasant summit. In many places the rock is covered with mosses and lichens. Blueberries and mountain cranberries grow along the perimeters of the clearing. Quartzite and mica schists glisten in the exposed rock. Mining for tourmaline and feldspar has taken place on the mountain. For many years this region of Maine has been renowned for its extensive deposits of precious stones. What appears to be the world's largest tourmaline deposit was discovered nearby in recent years.

When you're ready to head down, retrace your steps carefully. avoid getting thrown off course by the many side roads and intersecting tracks both on the summit and lower down.

6

Burnt Meadow Mountain

Distance (round trip): 2½ miles

Hiking time: 2½ hours

Vertical rise: 1,100 feet

Map: USGS 7½' Brownfield

Burnt Meadow Mountain offers hikers a fine walk, excellent views, and, most likely, plenty of solitude in west central Maine, near the New Hampshire state line. Burnt Meadow is one of those interesting but not-much-climbed massifs that, looking like great, half-risen loaves of bread, run north and south along the western fringes of the Pine Tree State in a kind of solitary splendor. With its three distinctive peaks, Burnt Meadow provides some marvelous sight lines over several dozen other hills that straddle this border country, including New Hampshire's Presidentials. Although this walk is not many miles from the wearying commercial hubbub of what is called "Mount Washington Valley," it might as well be in another world, and therein lies part of its appeal.

A major fire swept Burnt Meadow in 1947, accounting for its young forestation, mainly deciduous woods, and considerable exposed granitic ledge. This young forest makes a pleasant change from the often-encountered dense coniferous forest in evidence on many Maine trails, and, if you hike in late autumn or early spring with the trees bare of leaves, the views on this walk are even more spectacular. The route crosses no brooks or streams, so bring along plenty of water in your rucksack.

It takes a little back-road navigating to reach the trailhead on Burnt Meadow's east side. From the junction of ME 113 and ME 160 by a general store in Brownfield, drive west through the village on ME 160 for a little over a mile until the road makes a sharp left by the community church. Con-

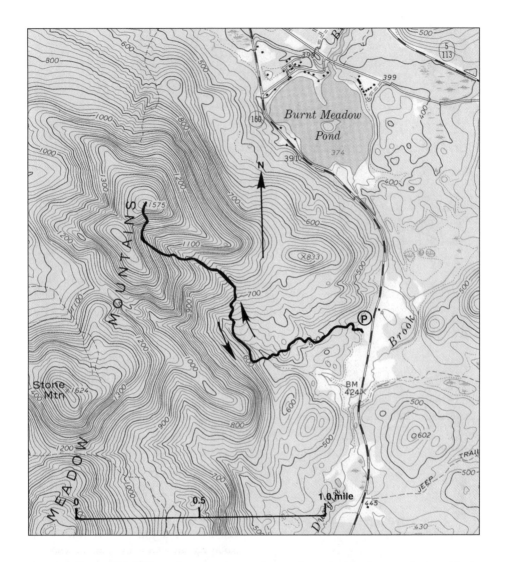

tinue south on ME 160 past a cemetery and go by Burnt Meadow Pond. Two miles south of the church you'll find a metal sign indicating FIRE ROAD 145 on your right, where there's a shady turnout. Park here.

The trail, which is not visible from the road, leaves the turnout under a canopy of red and white pine and white birch, climbing the first of many ledgy outcrops dotted with haircap moss. Follow the blue blazes upward through a series of esses toward the southwest amid clumps of ground juniper and desiccated lichens. More open ledge is reached shortly, with the first easterly views from the trail. Here and there are veins of quartzite and mica schist embedded in the host granite. A panorama of rolling green mountains gradually comes into view in a line from the southeast to the northeast.

The trail rises more gradually in groves of white oak, one of the deciduous species

Burnt Meadow Mountain

characteristic of this hike over once-burned ground. You pass a patch of common louse-wort, and views to the north open up over your shoulder. Meandering more and more southwest, walk onto a second series of open ledges with more expansive views. Staghorn sumac and limited red spruce are seen. In minutes, you reach a fine, open bluff with broad views to the valleys and mountains southward.

From this bluff, follow the trail sharply around to the north and northwest as it ascends steadily through mixed hard-woods. Bearberry, goldenrod, and ground blueberries grow profusely along the path. Pass a pair of young hemlocks; the trail bears right and then left in a small clearing. Though it will probably be gone by the time you walk this path, I have seen here one of the largest hornets' nests I've ever come across in the woods. This one, probably made by yellow jackets or paper wasps and attached to a young cherry sapling, was the size of a football inflated to twice normal size. So elaborate and complex are these engineering marvels that it is hard to believe that they are used only one season and then abandoned, a new nest being constructed next season.

Beyond this bend a ledge takes you up and westward into a clearing bordered by mountain ash, hemlock, red spruce, white pine, and sumac; the ground is covered with weathered lichen. Excellent views to the south, perhaps 40 miles into the distance on a clear day, open up as you proceed on near-level ground. Clumps of bearberries lie along the path now. The route rises again to the southwest and west.

Occasional glimpses of the second major hummock you'll climb on this hike appear to the northwest as the trail pulls rightward, crosses another level spot, passes a row of hemlocks, and descends past several large boulders deposited here as glacial erratics. The trail runs through a slump filled with spindly young ash, birch, and beech, and then rises very steadily west and northwest to more ledges with good views to your left (south).

The scramble over the middle hummock now begins as the route runs through ever shorter vegetation and out onto open ledge bordered by thick dwarf oak. Ground blue-berries grow profusely all around, separated by clumps of ground juniper. The main summit rises to the northwest. With the exception of a few wind-beaten pines, vegetation here is low, shaped by the prevailing winds that come up from the valleys to the south. You can see far into the distance—from the south-west all the way around to the north. I ob-served a variety of birds when last here. Four pairs of ravens (Corvus corax principalis) made soft quorking sounds as they rode the thermals near the summit.

The trail now runs northwest continu-ously, making the last steep rise to the sum-mit. Scramble up a series of fractured granitic ledges. Black-capped chickadees flit about a small stand of spruce. A final turn through the ledges brings you up onto the summit, where, by looking back toward the southeast, you can see the two hum-mocks you have traversed and, well out to the east, the road where you parked.

This is a broad, flat, open summit with mountainous views in all directions except northwest and north (views to the north are possible in spring, late fall, and winter, when the mainly deciduous cover is bare). In summer, sounds drift lazily up from Burnt Meadow Pond, which lies to the east be-low. A narrow, grassy road meanders downward from the summit's north side, a remnant of the days when this mountain had a ski area on its northern slopes, now thankfully gone.

Though not a killer climb, Burnt Meadow offers mountain views from its 1,600-foot summit that rival those of some of the more demanding hikes in this region. There are many pleasant spots around the summit to rest and picnic while enjoying the splendid outlooks, especially to the south, where there is very little sign of human intrusion beyond a few scattered farms.

To the southeast, you can easily see the route you traversed on the ascent and will now retrace. Dropping down into the trees again, you'll reach the road in 45 minutes of steady walking.

7

Miles Notch–Great Brook Loop

Distance (around loop): 11 miles

Hiking time: 7½ hours

Vertical rise: 2,150 feet

*Maps: USGS 7½' Speckled Mountain;
AMC Carter–Mahoosuc sheet*

For the enthusiastic, long-distance hiker, the walk in to Miles Notch and the circuit of the major summits that lie to its west make one of the finest day trips in Maine's mountains. Located in the little-visited lands east of the Evans Notch region and north of Kezar Lake, this extended, horseshoe-shaped route provides excellent, seldom seen views over many western Maine mountains and New Hampshire's Presidentials. These hills also have the virtue of being infrequently walked, and it's rare to meet anyone on the trail, especially if you hike midweek.

Hikers who set out on this route should be fit, experienced trail users. The first half of the route is well marked and easy to follow. Portions of the second half from Butters Mountain to the Great Brook Trail junction are brushy, not well marked, and require a good sense of direction and the ability to locate a sometimes barely discernible footpath. (Trail maintenance *may* have improved this section since this description was written.) You should definitely carry a map (USGS Speckled Mountain 7½-minute series or AMC Carter-Mahoosuc sheet) and compass. Although there are brooks near the trail on the first and last thirds of the route, you should not count on finding potable water anywhere on this walk in a dry summer. Carry plenty of fluids and food with you.

You can approach the trail from either north or south on ME 5. Turn west off ME 5 in North Lovell by the Evergreen Valley sign. Follow this road toward Evergreen Valley for approximately 1.75 miles and make a

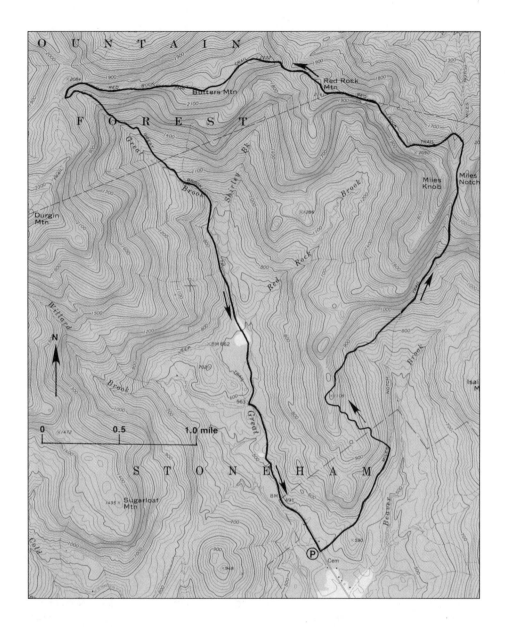

sharp right onto Hut Road. Follow Hut Road as it meanders north and northwest along the lower reaches of Great Brook and past some cottages. About 3 miles from ME 5, the road arches around to your left and becomes gravel surfaced. You pass several houses here and go by a cem-etery to your left. A short distance farther on you'll see the Miles Notch Trail sign on your right opposite a grassy parking turn-out. Leave your car here.

The Miles Notch Trail, the first leg of this extended hike, is an attractive, wooded path that connects, on its north end, with the Haystack Notch Trail (see also Hike 28) in some unspoiled backcountry in West Bethel. From the signpost at the trailhead, walk east-northeast into brushy woodlands on a grown-up tote road. Ash, beech, young maples, and red oaks lie on both sides of the trail. They are typical of the cover you will see on a large part of this walk. The area was cut over perhaps 10 or 12 years ago and has since come back in this young, deciduous cover. The beeches are numerous all over this area, and the "mast" crop that they drop from their branches at season's end accounts for this being a favorite black bear territory.

The trail rises quickly into some towering white pines and soon parallels the west bank of seasonal Beaver Brook. Little clumps of arborvitae dot the ground, and you cross a bar of granitic ledge shortly. The trail continues to follow the bed of the tote road as it works its way generally northward. Nearly a mile from the trailhead, a big log blocks the road, and mustard yellow blazes direct you left (west) along a rerouting of the old trail. Walking west and northwest here on what is not a very distinct path, you crest a small rise by a glacial erratic topped with woodferns.

Your walk continues to drift northwest in the direction of a ridge for a while. In a grove of more white pines, the trail pulls toward the east-northeast at the base of the ridge. You need to watch for blazes carefully to spot this turn. Passing some tall white birches, the trail quickly begins to lead you up some granitic ledges, still in a northeasterly direction. Views to the west toward Speckled and Durgin Mountains open up; they're best in spring and autumn. Topping the ridge among stands of oak, pass through a grove of red pine and begin a march toward the east and northeast. You'll pass a number of granite outcrops and

walk through very attractive groves of red spruce and, later, aged hemlock.

The trail continues, dropping downward to the east-northeast, and rejoins the tote road at a point roughly 1½ miles above the left turn you made earlier. Following the roadbed northward, work your way up the steepening cleft between Elizabeth Mountain (still identified as Miles Knob on some maps) and, to the east, Isaiah Mountain. The great, overhanging granitic cliffs of Elizabeth Mountain come gradually into view to your left, and you cross Beaver Brook as you head again northeastward.

The walk on the final rise to the col that leads to Elizabeth Mountain can be rather steep in places and demands steady effort. Fragrant woodfern, northern maidenhair, and lady fern grow along the route. The trail climbs along the spruce- and lichen-covered side of Peter Mountain, where a sign indicates the Red Rock Trail to your left. Turn left (west) here and descend into a gully—which you go straight across—then commence a climb up the north side of Elizabeth Mountain. (From the point of leaving the Miles Notch Trail, the route west is not blazed and at some places you may lose the path. Watch carefully.) You now climb on steady grades west and southwest through stands of beech, where there are occasional good outlooks north and northeast. The trail crests Elizabeth Mountain and begins to meander northwest through groves of spruce and balsam, where it drops into a gully and rises again. At 1¼ miles from the Miles Notch Trail, you emerge on the ledgy summit ridge of Red Rock Mountain. There are fine views both north and south along here, and the most beautiful portion of the walk lies in the next 1½ miles. Watch for a turnout to your left where there is a good spot to picnic, with majestic outlooks over Kezar Lake to the south.

Miles Notch Trailhead

Continuing westward along the ridge, you pass many open spots with splendid views. The imposing summit to the northwest is Caribou Mountain in Evans Notch (see Hike 29), with Haystack Mountain just visible to its left. You come to a couple of points where, looking carefully west-southwest, you can see the summit of New Hampshire's Mount Washington just visible between foreground peaks. In a few minutes you'll pass a last open ledge, with fine views to Butters Mountain and southwest to Speckled Mountain, and descend into another gully. In the low ground, cross the seasonal headwaters of Shirley Brook, then clamber up to the flat ridge of Butters Mountain. More views are available here over what is largely wild country. Haystack Notch is immediately below to the north.

Once past the open summit area, the trail on Butters Mountain slabs west-south-west, staying not far below the ridge and coming back up onto the ridge from time to time. Views diminish, and the trail becomes brushy and is often blocked by fallen trees. In this section, the trail can be very hard to follow and even experienced hikers will need to use care (more recent trail work, if any, may improve this situation). The route gradually pulls around to the south toward Durgin and Speckled Mountains and arrives, in a glade dense with ferns, at the Great Brook trailhead.

Bear left on this yellow-blazed trail and commence the descent on the last leg of the loop. Walk east on level ground for a short way with some layered granite slabs to your left. The ridge you walked earlier can also be seen to your left. The route soon plunges down to the southeast, losing more than 1,000 feet of altitude in the next mile. Attractive views to the valley southward open up from time to time. The trail drops steadily, staying to the north of Great Brook, and crosses both Shirley Brook and Red Rock Brook. Great Brook is just a trickle of water in high summer, but in late winter and spring, snowmelt courses down here in great torrents; the much widened, ledgy falls over which the brook passes are on your right.

About 2 miles below the trail junction at a Wilderness Area boundary post, cross Great Brook. A short distance farther down, the path pulls away from the brook and southward on a grassy tote road. The terrain flattens some and walking becomes pleasantly easy here. Stay with the yellow blazes as the tote road widens and the trail proceeds south and southeast on a network of connecting, little-used woods roads. Walk this terrain for another ½ mile, where you join a wider, gravel road and shortly pass over a gated wooden bridge. Continue the walk southeastward now, past several campsites and side roads. In another mile, you reach the parking area and trailhead where you began the walk.

II

South Coast and Camden Hills

8

Dodge Point Circuit, Damariscotta

Distance (around loop): 2½ miles

Hiking time: 2 hours

Vertical rise: 230 feet

Maps: USGS 7½' Bristol; Maine Bureau of Public Lands Dodge Point map

A quiet hike through majestic pines along the shore of an attractive river: That's what you'll find when you walk the 500-acre Dodge Point preserve near the pretty village of Newcastle in the heart of coastal Maine. Though not far from the town centers of both Newcastle and Damariscotta, Dodge Point is a world unto itself, beautifully forested, tranquil, and rich with varied plant and animal life. A developed network of trails runs through the preserve and offers fine walking on easy grades. In winter, snowshoeing and cross-country skiing are welcome sports here as well.

Dodge Point was acquired by the Land for Maine's Future Board from the Edward Freeman Trust in 1989. The Maine Bureau of Public Lands and the Maine Coastal Access Program spearheaded the acquisition, with funding provided by the Land for Maine's Future Program, the Damariscotta River Association, and the Maine Coastal Program. The Damariscotta River Association currently supports the management and maintenance of the preserve. The Bureau of Public Lands also encourages educational and research uses here.

Dodge Point lies on River Road, south of its intersection with US 1 in Newcastle. From the large church in Newcastle Square, head south on River Road for 3.5 miles, watching for a well-marked parking area on your left. The hike may also be approached from the south. Drive north on ME 27 (River Road) 9.5 miles from Booth-bay. Leave your car here at the trailhead, where an information board will acquaint you with the trail network.

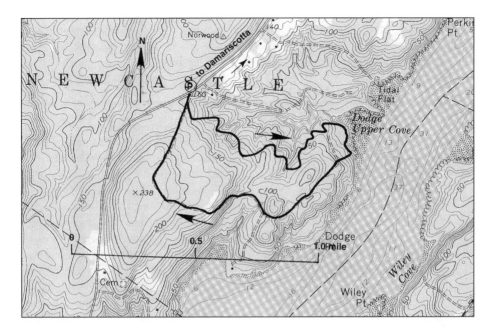

This route makes a 2½-mile circuit of the coastal side of the reserve, following the Ravine Trail and Old Farm Road. Walk first through the gate of Old Farm Road and continue south for a few steps, immediately bearing left (southeast) on the Ravine Trail. Walk through white pine, birch, and balsam cover. Small clumps of arborvitae, polypody fern and lady fern grow at the edges of the path. You hike up and down here over little ribs of buried rock as the route pulls around shortly to the east and northeast. You'll pass stands of red oaks and white birch. Some old pines look as if they had been ruinously explored by woodpeckers, and others have been stripped of their bark by porcupines. Certainly one of the pleasures of this walk is the interesting and constantly changing mixture of tree growth in this very attractive climax forest.

The forest canopy is higher and more open now. Christmas ferns grow under an overstory of lofty white pines. Pulling to the southeast again, the trail drops into a little spruce-filled depression and crosses a tiny, seasonal brook. Some minor twists and turns come next as the unblazed trail pulls northeast and then around to the east. Watch carefully to stay on the path. After passing some bits of sedimentary and granitic rock, the trail descends slightly and arrives at a fine old stone wall, where it turns abruptly to the south on a mossy right-of-way. The path now follows the stone wall for a short distance with big, hardrock maples on your right and stands of tall white pines on your left. Ledgy outcrops are exposed beneath the maples. Here the path is roughly 100 feet above sea level, an elevation that soon will be lost as you make your way toward the river.

After walking about 70 yards along this right-of-way, bear left into the woods and go southeast in a grove of tall pines. The trail emerges in a stand of red oaks, white oaks, and maples and runs eastward with a deepening ravine on your left. The ravine collects runoff from its surrounding area, forms a stream, and the captured water flows northeastward to Ice Pond. Staying close to the ravine, the trail gradually pulls to the northeast and enters the fringes of a great red pine plantation that dominates much of the point. Within minutes, you turn eastward along the shore of Ice Pond. Crossing a ditch, pick up Old Farm Road, turn right, and follow it through a grove to the nearby shore of the Damariscotta River.

By a cove and stream that connect with Ice Pond, you come to Brickyard Beach. Here you'll find excellent views upriver toward Damariscotta and downriver toward Wiley Point. Prentiss Island in South Bristol lies directly across the river. Although intervening headlands block the view, the river runs southward to the Gulf of Maine through Edgecomb, South Bristol, and Boothbay.

More than 11,000 years ago, the Damariscotta River was formed by the retreating glacial ice sheet, which gouged its streambed. Archaeological research indicates that Native Americans resided, hunted, and fished along these shores as early as 500 B.C. The river's name, "a place of many little fishes" in Abenaki, was derived from spring runs of spawning alewives farther up the river at Damariscotta Mills. A tidal river, the Damariscotta is flushed by Atlantic tides that mingle with fresh water above, in Great Salt Bay. Southward, where the river empties into the Gulf of Maine, lies Damariscove Island, site of the first (ill-fated) attempt to establish an overwintering settlement in New England. You will find old, broken bricks lying along the shore. The local clay once supported over twenty brick foundaries in this river basin.

From Brickyard Beach, walk through the grove and back up to Old Farm Road. Turn left and follow the road as it rises southward, passing the Shore Trail on your left,

to a junction in a clearing. Keep right and walk to the southwest here as the road meanders through beautiful, tall stands of red pine. This plantation was begun in 1928, and further plantings continued through 1940.

You'll soon pass a firebreak on your right; continue southwest, climbing gradually. Links to the Shore Trail lead off to your left at two points along this stretch. Vegetation begins to change now. White pines, maples, and white birch characterize the next section of the route as you hike westward on steeper grades toward the highest point on this circuit. An old stone wall lies to your left. In minutes, the road broadens and passes an old shack on your right.

Many birds visit Dodge Point in-season, from the smaller species usually associated with this type of northern forest to bald eagles and osprey, which enjoy the point's proximity to good fishing grounds. As I walked along this section of the trail one recent winter day, a great flapping sound drew my attention to a bald eagle launching itself into the wind from a tree directly overhead. I wished I had been observant enough to spot it sooner, but I followed the bird's majestic flight southeastward with my binoculars. Hardly the kind of experience one soon forgets.

Leading through more red pine forest, Old Farm Road continues westward on a densely wooded plateau about 230 feet above the river's level, crossing the highest point on the hike. A stone wall appears on your left, and the road pulls sharply to your right (north). The grassy track passes several woods roads, which come in from left and right. The remains of stone walls now lie attractively on both sides of the road, overgrown by vines and brush. Continuing northward through pretty, mixed-growth forest, you walk the widening road as it de-

Red pine groves, Dodge Point

scends slowly, passes the Ravine Trail you entered earlier, and ends at the parking area.

Note: Hikers may also wish to add the self-guiding nature walk along the Shore Trail to their explorations. The Shore Trail departs Old Farm Road in several places. Maggie Macy-Peterson's excellent self-guide to this separate nature walk, entitled *The Discovery Trail at Dodge Point,* is for sale at the Skidompha Library on Main Street in Damariscotta, or by writing to the Damariscotta River Association, P.O. Box 333, Damariscotta, ME 04543. Memberships in the association are also available; call 207-563-1393.

9

Mount Battie

Distance (round trip): 1 mile

Hiking time: 1 hour

Vertical rise: 600 feet

Map: USGS 7½' Camden

Later in this book, I describe some of the exceptional climbing and hiking on Mount Desert Island. Mount Desert boasts the highest peaks along the North Atlantic seaboard and views to match. But because Maine is Maine, there happens to be a second excellent area of coastal hiking near what many consider the finest yachting harbor in the East. Camden, long recognized as the place "where the mountains come down to the sea," is the center of a ring of pleasant, low mountains that provide good hiking and views nearly comparable to those of Mount Desert.

A good first hike in the area, Mount Battie offers short, steep routes to exceptional views of the Camden coastal scene. The Mount Battie South Trail rises from the northwest residential section of Camden, not far from the business district. The trail is reached by turning west onto ME 52 from its junction with US 1, just north of the town square. Take the first right, which is Megunticook Street, and follow it to a small parking space at the base of the mountain.

The trail starts behind a grand old Victorian house at the top of Megunticook Street. It's the house with the prominent widow's walk and the huge boulders in the front yard. A small parking space lies behind the house at the trailhead. Please be careful not to trespass on the grounds of the houses bordering this area and not to block the driveways.

The trail leads north from the parking area, climbing steeply up through mixed growth away from the houses. A series of esses are walked, with the trail rising

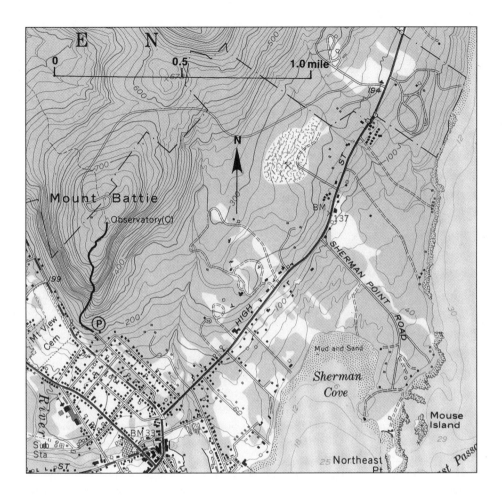

steadily in the direction of the summit to the north. Deciduous growth gives way to red and white pine cover. Boulders, broken off from ledges above, are scattered about. The woods begin to thin out, and views to the south open up. Looping around a ledgy outcrop, the trail winds upward, climbing out of the trees and onto a series of ledges that will characterize the rest of the walk. Pulling first to the left over exposed ledge, the trail winds westward briefly. A plateau is crossed, and the walk to the summit resumes with a quick scramble that will have you puffing. In minutes, the last rise is topped and

you walk up through the low scrub to the bare summit. The whole walk up from the road has been just over ½ mile, but will seem longer due to the steep rise. The views here fully compensate your effort.

The outlook from Mount Battie's sprawling summit is superb, rivaled only by Ocean Lookout (see Hike 12, Mount Megunticook). On clear days, Vinalhaven, North Haven, and Isle au Haut are visible, as are other islands along the midcoast. A stone tower marks Battie's highest point, and you'll see a bit more from its platform than you will from the many ground-level viewing

On the summit of Mount Battie, overlooking Camden Harbor

spots scattered around the summit. (If you look northwest from the tower, you'll see Ocean Lookout on Mount Megunticook and the long, east–west ledgy flanks of Megunticook itself.)

Legend has it that American poet Edna St. Vincent Millay came up here often to think and to write. The spot is assumed to be the inspiration for her lyric *Renascence*. A nice look around the summit can be had by walking around the loop made by the summit road. There are excellent views to the north as you stroll along and perhaps find inspiration of your own.

10

Cameron Mountain

Distance (round trip): 6⅓ miles

Hiking time: 3½ hours

Vertical rise: 700 feet

Maps: USGS 7½' Lincolnville; Camden Hills State Park map; AMC map

Cameron Mountain rests in the second rank of Camden Hills. Not among those that line US 1 and directly front the ocean, Cameron lies back in the woods behind the first range and orients itself more to the country toward the west. Away from the bustle of Camden Harbor, Cameron Mountain makes a pleasant elevation for taking the measure of the Camden highlands and for enjoying the bright, high breezes of a summer day out of earshot of tourist traffic. If you hike as a family, this route is good for children over 6 or 7, as the grades are very moderate.

This attractive jaunt into the country on the west side of Camden Hills State Park is longer than it once was. For many years, you could drive rough Ski Lodge Road right to the trailhead. Happily the road is now gated and free of vehicular traffic, and this quiet walk begins farther out on ME 173 in Lincolnville. You may wish to pick up a map of Camden Hills State Park at park headquarters just north of Camden center on US 1. There is also an Appalachian Mountain Club (AMC) map of these hills, which shows somewhat more detail than the park map. It can be found in local bookstores. Then drive 4 miles farther north on US 1 to Lincolnville and turn west onto ME 173, continuing 2.3 miles to a fork in the road. Bear left on Youngtown Road and immediately left again into the park service parking lot at the trailhead. A bulletin board with trail announcements stands here.

Go through the gate and follow the gravel Ski Lodge Road southeast, then southwest as it rises slowly on comfortable

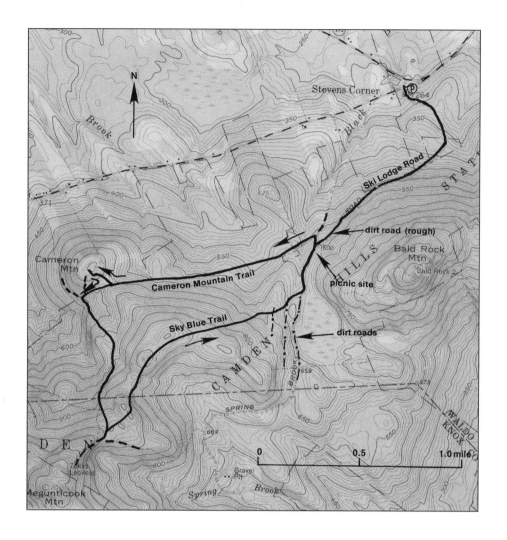

grades. This road now is much more tranquil and pleasant to walk than when it was frequently churned to a fine mud by off-road-vehicle drivers. Park rangers have performed a real service to hikers by gating this right-of-way.

The road proceeds through high, deciduous forest thick with maple, red and white oak, beech, red spruce, and ash. Great, older trees arch over the road, which continues to climb steadily. At 1⅓ miles

from your starting place, you reach the old Heald picnic area, which lies on your left under a stand of tall white pines. A trail also departs eastward here for Bald Rock Mountain (see Hike 13). Directly *opposite* this picnic grove you'll see a narrow, grassy road descending northward into the woods. Head down this road a short distance until, on your left, you come upon Cameron Mountain Trail, which is signed.

Bear left onto this trail and follow it

South Coast and Camden Hills

The view northeast from Cameron Mountain

southwest as it rises gently between crumbling stone walls, old cellar holes, and abandoned orchards. The walk here is through very pretty climax forest, grown thick with brush on the north side and dotted with lady fern and silver glade fern. Climbing comfortably, you soon cross Black Brook on a rather rickety old plank bridge that has seen better days. The stone wall disappears and then reappears as you crest a final rise and, through a gap in the wall, see the nublike summit of Cameron Mountain in a blueberry field to your right.

You can reach the summit by a short march up an obvious cart track. (The summit is on private land, where blueberries are harvested commercially, so please leave no trace of your passing.) A farm pasture once occupied this place, but nature has reclaimed much of it. Other than the blueberries, the field now boasts only wildflowers such as meadowsweet, daisies, black-eyed

Susans, and yarrow as its crop. Excellent views to the southwest, west, and north are yours from the summit cairn. Levenseller Mountain in Searsmont is seen to the northwest, and Gould Hill rises to the north over Coleman Pond. Bald Rock Mountain is close by to the east, and 1,200-foot Mount Megunticook (Hike 12) is the long ridge due south. Hatchet Mountain and Moody Mountain form the north–south ridge that connects with Levenseller Mountain. The pretty valleys to the west are sprinkled with small farms.

Once off the summit of Cameron, go *right* on the Cameron Mountain Trail again and descend southwestward for a short distance. Watch carefully for a narrow, grassy road that bears sharply left (southeast). A small sign indicates SKI LODGE ROAD. Make the left described and walk uphill on moderate grades. This continuation of the trail will bring you up onto a connecting

Cameron Mountain

ridge. The deciduous growth that has characterized the route thus far begins to give way to conifers, dominated by densely grown balsam and black spruce. The walking here has an attractive, alpine flavor not seen below.

Pulling next around to the south, the Cameron Mountain Trail rises higher and connects with the Sky Blue Trail at a height-of-land about a mile from where you left the blueberry field. You must look carefully for this junction. There is a lone sign on a tree to your left that's easily missed.

The Sky Blue Trail has few open views but meanders through superbly attractive country. Here you'll walk north and northwest through groves of black spruce and over a series of ledgy, open pastures. You'll pass several large granite outcrops on both left and right, and the route will pull gradually eastward, descending steadily. The right-of-way is marked occasionally with granite cairns. The path is less obvious to winter walkers and snowshoers; it's quite possible, in snow, to wander off at the trail's various turnings, resulting in some unplanned bushwhacks. A bit over a mile from the junction, a couple of tote roads enter from your right, one of which joins the trail. A short distance farther on, you emerge on the broader gravel of Ski Lodge Road and bear left.

To make the walk out to your car, proceed north and northeast on Ski Lodge Road. In ⅓ mile you'll pass the picnic area and the path opposite where you earlier gained the Cameron Mountain Trail. Continue to retrace your steps northeastward on Ski Lodge Road, and you'll reach the trailhead and parking area in another 1 ⅓ miles.

11

Maiden Cliff Loop

Distance (around loop): 2¼ miles

Hiking time: 2 hours

Vertical rise: 700 feet

Maps: USGS 7½' Camden; USGS 7½' Lincolnville

If sheer cliffs and picture-postcard panoramas appeal to you, the climb up Maiden Cliff, west of Camden, has something to offer both you and your camera. The cliff proves that some of the best views in the Camden hills are inland. Looming high over Megunticook Lake, Maiden Cliff—less romantically known as the Millerite Ledges—furnishes striking views to the south, west, north, and down on the extensive waters of the lake itself.

To reach the trailhead, take ME 52 west from Camden. Just before the road begins bordering the lake, 3 miles from US 1, a small, raised parking area, known as the Barrett Farm site, lies above the road on your right. Leave your car here and head north-northwest across the field into the woods. The trail follows an old logging road on a gradual rise through groves of beech and birch. The trail turns more northeasterly soon, and you walk above, and parallel to, a westward-running brook.

You cross the brook shortly on a weathered log bridge and climb to your left up the bed of another seasonal brook, going northward. Pulling into hemlock woods to the right of this second brook, the trail climbs around to the northeast, rising steadily in more coniferous forest. It's cool and shady here in summer. You arrive, about ½ mile above the road, at a well-marked trail junction.

Go right at the junction and climb first easterly, then north as the trail ascends quickly onto the higher ground of the ridge. You are headed toward what the marker below calls a scenic trail junction with the

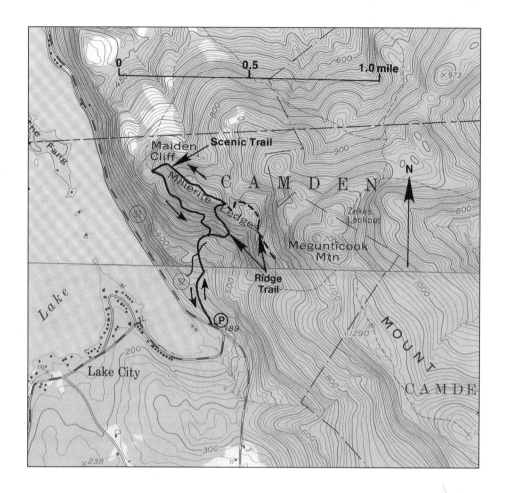

Ridge Trail. As you ascend, there are open spots to the left of the trail with excellent views toward the southernmost Camden Hills. Pulling steeply northeast again, you emerge upon some open ledges with views eastward along Megunticook Ridge and over to Mount Battie. On a clear day, you'll see a good stretch of open ocean down toward Rockport and Rockland.

Continue a bit higher and you'll spot a junction marker where you bear sharply left (northwest) on the Scenic Trail. Follow this path over more high, exposed ledge and through the occasional slump as it meanders over the rock toward Maiden Cliff. The

views here are spectacular to the southwest and northwest, and there are a number of excellent, open places to picnic and take the sun in mild weather. The white blazes lead along the edge of the ledges and eventually curve downward to the west, where they lead to Maiden Cliff. The open cliffs are just beyond a trail junction, slightly off to your right through a grove.

A metal cross above the plunging cliffs marks the point where 11-year-old Eleanora French fell to her death in May 1864. Below you to the west lies Megunticook Lake. Bald and Ragged Mountains are to the southwest. Norton

---

South Coast and Camden Hills

Looking northwest from Maiden Cliff

and Coleman Ponds lie to the northwest, beyond the lake. Far to the south, you can see the ocean.

To return to the road, go back to the junction of the Scenic Trail and the Maiden Cliff Trail, which you passed minutes before. Go south on the Maiden Cliff Trail, walking first over fairly level ground, then ascending a series of steps. The predomi-nantly deciduous forest of the upper slope gives way gradually to the conifers of the lower ground as you walk back to the trail junction first passed on your way in. The junction is reached in less than ½ mile, and you bear right (southwest), following the bed of the brook toward your car. Retrace your steps over the footbridge and along the woods road to the parking area.

12

Mount Megunticook

Distance (round trip): 5¼ miles

Hiking time: 4 hours

Vertical rise: 1,190 feet

Maps: USGS 7½' Camden; USGS 7½' Lincolnville

A good part of the Camden area's best hiking lies within Camden Hills State Park, which provides well-managed camping facilities at the very base of the mountain trails network. The park camping area is on US 1, about 2 miles north of Camden town center. The park office will provide you, upon request, with a good map of the local trails that will suggest other walks to complement those we have included here.

The broad ridge running from Maiden Cliff in the northwest to the state park campground in the southeast is Mount Megunticook. The mountain, highest in the Camden area and second highest on the northeast coast after Cadillac Mountain on Mount Desert Island, provides the best lookouts to the long expanse of Penobscot Bay. Ocean Lookout, about ⅓ mile east of the wooded, true summit, is your destination for this extended, 5-mile ridge walk.

Most hikers approach Megunticook from its busier east side. A quieter, longer, and highly scenic approach can be made from the west, and it's that hike we set out for here. To reach the trailhead, drive west on ME 52 from Camden center, parking at the Barrett Farm site on your right about 3 miles west of US 1.

This route follows the same trail from the north end of the parking area as does Hike 11, Maiden Cliff. The rise is along an old woods road that follows a brook past a giant boulder and up into the woods. About ½ mile north and northeast above the road, you reach a trail junction in a hemlock grove. Keep right here and climb northeast and north as the trail rises quickly to the

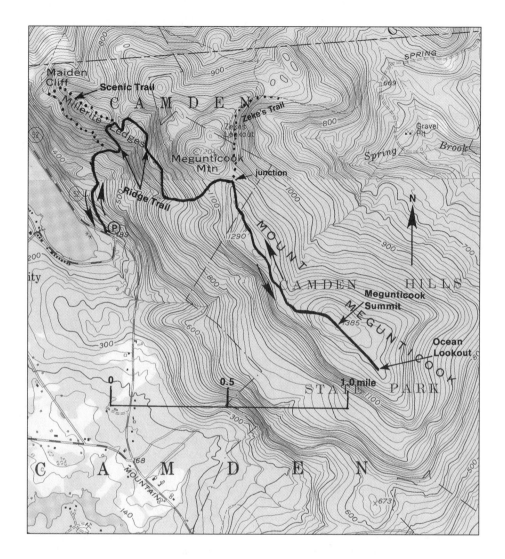

open ledges at another junction, where the Ridge Trail and the Scenic Trail meet. Pause here a moment to enjoy the fine views eastward. You can get a sense of the route ahead, for the long ridge of Megunticook stretches before you, and, off to the right a bit, you can see Mount Battie, with its distinctive stone tower.

From here on, the walk becomes more private. You drop eastward into mixed-growth forest, curving gradually northeast-

ward through low ground. The trail now begins to ascend a series of ribs as you start to gain altitude on the west flanks of Megunticook itself. The grades are not steep and your progress upward is steady. Deciduous hardwoods gradually give way to groves of hemlock, spruce, and balsam as you go higher. An hour and a half from the road (about 1 ⅓ miles), you arrive at a third trail junction in a shady hemlock stand. A trail runs north here toward Zeke's Look-

The east shoulder of Mount Megunticook

out, Cameron Mountain, and Bald Rock Mountain.

Keep right in this grove, however, and go east and southeast on the Megunticook Ridge Trail. In mainly coniferous woods, the trail rises gradually past a series of lookouts with open views across to Ragged and Bald Mountains. Just over 2¼ miles from your starting point, you reach Megunticook's wooded summit and a junction with the Slope Trail. Continue southeast and south now, walking the final ⅓ mile to Ocean Lookout.

Although the views along this walk are always fine, Ocean Lookout offers one of the best vantage points on the entire New England coast. Vinalhaven and North Haven are due east. Islesboro lies closer to shore in the northeast. Beyond Vinalhaven

are the low shapes of Deer Isle and the whaleback known as Isle au Haut. Southward are superb outlooks over Rockland and Thomaston and on down the coast. On a sunny day, regardless of the season, Ocean Lookout is a natural place of great beauty to rest a while and enjoy the fruits of your uphill stroll.

The return is made by retracing your steps westward, remembering to keep left at the junction of Zeke's Trail and left again when you reach the junction with the Scenic Trail. This round trip can be walked in four hours moving right along. Five hours, with plenty of time for lounging on the open ledges, is a more leisurely estimate. And bring binoculars. Ravens are always busy in the air along the ridge, and hawks are commonly sighted.

13

Bald Rock Mountain

Distance (round trip): 3½ miles

Hiking time: 2½ hours

Vertical rise: 800 feet

Maps: USGS 7½' Lincolnville; Camden Hills State Park map

This pretty, isolated mountain is at the northern end of Camden Hills State Park in the midst of the busy midcoast region. Bald Rock does not usually experience the heavy hiker use seen in those Camden hills that lie closer to the village. The woods around this 1,100-foot mountain make for varied and pleasant walking, and there are good ocean views from the summit. Because the approach is gradual, this route can be hiked by families with children over 6 or 7 years of age without difficulty. A full canteen belongs in your pack, for there are no springs along this trail.

The path to Bald Rock no longer leaves US 1 on the east side of the mountain, but now departs from a point northwest in Lincolnville. The trail from the east side has been logged and posted in recent years. To reach the new trailhead, drive to the junction of US 1 and ME 173 in Lincolnville (4 miles north of Camden center), turning west on ME 173. Follow this road to a junction, where you keep left. Just under a mile from this junction and 2.3 miles from US 1, bear left on Youngtown Road and immediately left again into a parking area that serves a network of trails. There is a trail information notice board here, and room to leave your car.

You begin by walking through the gate onto a shaded tote road that runs southeast and southwest on easy grades. This is the old Ski Lodge Road, more recently renamed Bald Rock Road, which runs well into the forest to the site of a now demolished building. In the past, the road has been open to seasonal vehicle traffic (usu-

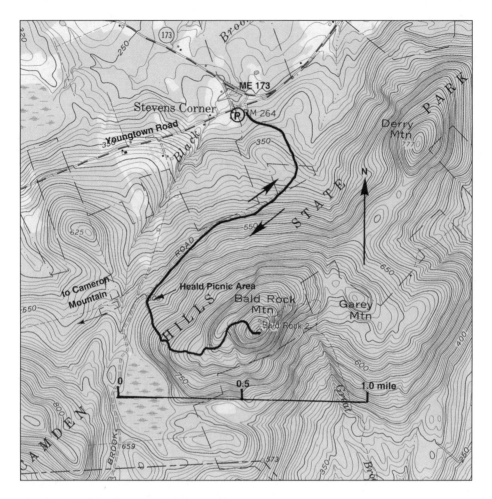

ally four-wheel-drive), but now it is likely to be closed to motorized travel in hiking season. Some parts of this route are open to trail-bikers. The mixed hardwoods near the trailhead gradually give way to conifers as the trail rises to about 600 feet above sea level.

As the grades level out, you reach a junction approximately 1⅓ miles from the parking area. Here, to your right, a trail leads to Cameron Mountain. To your left, you will head into the woods on a side trail to Bald Rock. Departing from a grove of tall conifers at what used to be the old Heald Picnic Site, the path now heads south and

east in attractive mixed growth. The trail follows an old, gravelly tote road that winds gradually upward through groves of pines. The route pulls slowly through a series of bends in pleasant cover. A series of ridges and hummocks are crossed as the route climbs quickly, gradually pulling around to the northeast and east. The trail climbs steadily, rising about 500 feet before it pulls around to the northeast in a grove of evergreens and reaches the summit and its magnificent cluster of open ledges.

The fine views from Bald Rock run north and south, taking in a grand sweep of the

Coastal islands from Bald Rock Mountain

midcoast. The outlook northeast toward Islesboro and North Islesboro is particularly good. Looking due east on clear days, you may see Deer Isle farther out. Hard to the southeast, you may be able to see North Haven and Vinalhaven and, behind them, Isle au Haut, weather permitting. There are good views, too, down the coastal strip toward Camden. Many smaller islands are usually visible in the northern reaches of Penobscot Bay, and it is useful to have a chart of the bay along to help with identification. On fine summer days, there are more sailing craft than you thought existed majestically plying these sheltered waters.

An old, rather decrepit shelter is adjacent to the ledges, but a tent will serve you better if you wish to camp here. To regain the road, retrace your steps westward and down to Ski Lodge Road, and then turn right (north) to the parking area.

Hikers may obtain a local Camden Hills State Park map that shows this hike and others in the area by stopping at the park gate on US 1, just north of Camden center.

14

Ragged Mountain

Distance (round trip): 3 miles

Hiking time: 2½ hours

Vertical Rise: 850 feet

Map: USGS 7½' Camden; Georges River Land Trust Map: Ragged Mountain section

Ragged Mountain is a dramatic, ledgy hump that rises over beautiful Mirror Lake west of Camden and Rockport. Its brushy summit and its rocky outcrops of golden, weathered granite catch the traveler's eye from ME 17, and views of the mountain over Mirror Lake are particularly fine. Like all of the Camden Hills, this mountain rises less than 1,500 feet from the surrounding coastal plain, but its excellent summit views are those of a seemingly much higher land-form. A day spent hiking here offers the same visual attractions of Maine's major peaks to the northwest and north, with the added incentive of expansive ocean views.

The trailhead lies on the north side of ME 17, about 2 miles west of the junction of ME 17 and ME 90 in West Rockport and 2 miles east of the South Hope General Store. Parking for several vehicles will be found here in a gravel lot by a trailboard.

The winding trail to Ragged descends immediately from the parking lot east-north-east into a spruce and balsam slump, goes over a seasonal brook, and crosses a stone wall and tote road all within its first 150 yards. The blue-blazed route continues north-northeast in mixed growth and then pulls north in oaks and pines with plentiful arborvitae growing along the verge.

You next cross a stone wall and then walk parallel to it, going over a knoll dotted with hardwoods. Step over another stone wall shortly and walk onto a ledge covered with patches of ground juniper. In autumn, winter and spring, with the trees devoid of foliage, you can see the steep mass of Ragged close by to the east from

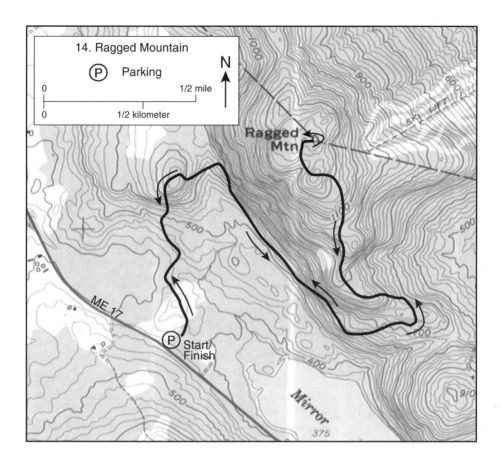

this spot. Drop north across a tote road next, going over another wall in white pines and spruce amid several mossy boulders.

Next, follow the blazes northwest up the spine of a little ridge in beech and ash cover. You pass along a line of silver birches and more beech, crossing a faint tote road in the open. Ascend a low ridge to the northeast now in more high-canopy hardwoods as you arrive under the west slope of Ragged Mountain.

The trail has been making a long northward loop around the boggy, low ground near Mirror Lake. The route now crosses a pretty stream and turns abruptly southeast under a massive rockfall. This looming cas-

cade of fragmented rock is testament to the work of frost in the cliffs above over many years. Standing here, you get the feeling that this isn't a place to hang around too long lest a missile from above come hurtling down. The path now heads through a thicket of cherry, alder, and zebrawood (striped birch). Soon you step over a little braided stream and pass several large boulders in stands of tall red oak. The stream you crossed earlier has widened and now flows southward to your right.

After less than 1/2 mile of progress to the southeast, the trail begins to draw away from the stream and ascends steeply upward to the east as views of Mirror Lake

Ragged Mountain over Mirror Lake

open under lofty old white pines. You can see beyond the lake across the coastal strip to the open Atlantic. Continuing upward, you climb onto an oak-studded ridge in a boulder field, the granite mammoths covered in rock tripe. Here you are standing in a saddle between Ragged's main summit and a subsidiary summit to the southeast. The trail next climbs quickly to the northwest, exposing dramatic, open panoramas of Spruce, Pleasant, and Meadow Mountains to the southwest.

Straddling the ridgeline, you now meander west and northwest over a series of ledges in groves of stunted oak. There are occasional spectacular views north and eastward toward Camden Harbor, Vinalhaven, and Isle au Haut here. You'll pass a number of lookouts as you make your way along the ridge. The cluttered summit of Ragged appears ahead in minutes, its terrain hosting several radio towers and relay

equipment. The best views are on the southeast side of the summit near the towers.

Ragged's 1,300-foot summit offers first-class outlooks down the Maine coast for more than 35 miles. On a clear afternoon you also can see the hills of Mount Desert Island far eastward up the coast and, in dry weather, the hills of western Maine and New Hampshire on the distant western horizon. Spruce and Pleasant Mountains rise boldly above Grassy Pond to the immediate west. Other Camden hills are visible to the east, left of Camden village, the long ridge of Mount Megunticook being the most prominent. On a fair day, you'll want to remain here for a while and, I'd guess, will be reluctant to leave.

The route down the mountain retraces your steps. Use caution on the summit ledges when the rock is wet. Watch the path closely as you descend southwest and then northwest along the feeder streams north of Mirror Lake. The pleasant, 3-mile round trip to Ragged's high ground and the return to the road can be completed in 2 and a half hours without hurrying.

Note: This hike is part of a new network of trails in the highlands west of Camden-Rockport created by the Georges River Land Trust. This trail network represents a refreshing way to explore this countryside and deserves accolades for the new opportunities the trails provide to hikers. Maps are generally available at trailheads or from the Georges River Land Trust, Studio 206, 328 Main Street, Rockland, ME 04841; 207-594-5166.

15

Bald Mountain

Distance (round trip): 2 miles

Hiking time: 1½ hours

Vertical Rise: 650 feet

Map: USGS 7½' Camden

There should be more trails like this interesting route up Bald Mountain in the beautiful Camden Hills. This path provides superb outlooks over the Camden highlands and out to the Atlantic from a breezy, open summit. The ascent is both short and undemanding with a couple of brief, steeper pitches along the way for variety. With a morning or afternoon free, you can't do better than a trip to the summit of Bald.

You'll find the Bald Mountain Trail on the Barnestown Road on Camden's west side. The road runs past the Camden Snow Bowl, and then negotiates a gap between Bald and Ragged Mountains, reaching the trailhead about 2 miles northwest of the ski area. A small parking lot on the east side of the road affords room to get your car off the pavement. A trail board offers current information.

The route drops quickly northeast on a boardwalk in a grove of alders and other mixed hardwoods. You walk through scattered red spruce and pine and come to an attractive stone wall on your left. In a few more yards, you cross a sweet little brook on a footbridge. Go further northeast amid a cluster of boulders and over a broken stone wall. You then pull more to the north in a shaded depression.

The trail next slabs across an arm of Bald Mountain to the northeast. In dense ash, oak, white, and silver birch growth, you have views back over your shoulder to the looming bulk of Ragged Mountain. Climbing rapidly, go through a little hemlock stand and follow the blue-blazed path as it turns sharply southeast. Watch for outlooks over nearby highland farms to the northwest and north. The

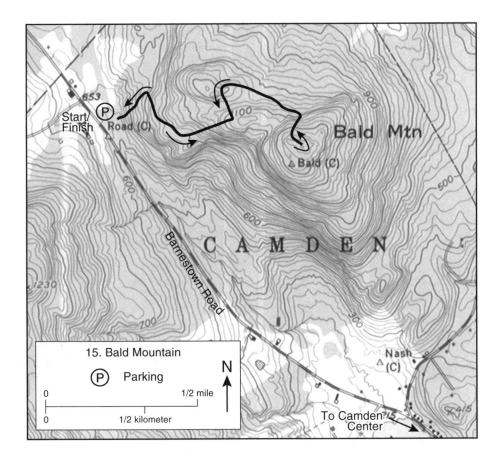

15. Bald Mountain

trail continues southeast through some rock-fall, leveling off somewhat in ground littered with arborvitae, and haircap and sphagnum mosses.

Dropping slightly, you follow the path as it next ascends a ledgy area and then abruptly turns east and northeast. The route turns to the southeast again shortly as it moves through young stands of beech. Crossing a tiny seasonal brook, you reach a clearing on ledgy, lichen-covered granite, where there are clusters of low-bush blueberries and fine views to westward. Outlooks toward the ocean to the south also begin to open up here. The entire ridgeline of Ragged Moun-

tain can be seen now, and you are roughly opposite Ragged's north summit.

The trail next pulls eastward on an arc with views ahead toward the summit. Opposite, the towered south peak of Ragged Mountain comes more clearly into view. Attractive Hosmer Pond lies to the southeast. Despite the steepness of the terrain, there is often a lot of deer sign hereabouts. The trail continues over a series of granite bars and runs briskly up a subsidiary ridge in scrub oaks, where you can see beyond the coastal strip to open ocean. The spindly trees also begin to yield outlooks inland to the northwest and west.

Bald Mountain from the southeast

Some cairns appear. There are signs of former blueberry cultivation here, not uncommon on the high, rolling hills of Maine's coastal region. You shortly reach a grassy dome where you have superb outlooks over village steeples to the north. The trail now pulls southeast in scrub oak with the wooded crown of the mountain ahead. Within sight, the pine-studded cliffs of Bald Mountain's west flank plunge to the valley before you. Throughout this section you'll have excellent views to the northeast, too.

Going through taller red oaks, you pass the loop trail on the right and continue rather steeply upward in dense spruce. The path zigzags toward higher ground on what may be slippery turf. You can look back here over the dome you have just crossed. Walk southwestward around the summit

dome in red spruce, ground juniper, lichens, and blueberries. Fine views of rolling countryside and inland farms in terrain dotted with ponds greet the eye here. Turning left, the trail ascends bare ledge steeply to the east and arrives on a granite slab grown up here and there with sedge and lichens. Beyond this shelf, through the opening in the evergreens, you reach another granite dome topped by a large, imposing cairn. This is the summit of Bald.

The north and northwest sides of this crown are topped with spruce, but in all other directions there are splendid open perspectives, the most direct being those eastward over Camden Harbor to the ocean and coastal islands of Vinalhaven and North Haven. Rockport Harbor lies to the southeast. You are able to see well up the coast here in the direction of Lincolnville, too. If you walk around you'll be able to spot Megunticook Ridge to the northeast. The summit of Bald is usually a breezy place, but find shelter and enjoy a rest and, perhaps, some refreshment before retracing your steps carefully to the valley.

Note: The trail you ascended is part of the Georges Highland Path and is maintained by the Georges River Land Trust. A local map may be available at the trailhead. For further information, contact: The Georges River Land Trust, 328 Main Street, Rockland, ME 04841; 207-594-5166.

Introduction

Of all the routes open to the inveterate hiker in Maine, few are in so different and dramatic a setting as those on Monhegan Island. With its tiny sister island, Manana, Monhegan lies 10 miles southeast of Pemaquid Point and 12 miles south of Port Clyde in the open Atlantic. The island is reached by passenger boat daily (in summer, thrice daily) from Port Clyde (the *Laura B or Elizabeth Ann*), from Shaw's Wharf in New Harbor via Hardy Boat (twice daily in summer) and, in summer only, from Boothbay Harbor (the *Balmy Days II*).

About 1 mile wide and 1¾ miles long, Monhegan is a community of artists and fishermen, numbering fewer than 100 in winter. The island population swells in summer and, at the time of writing, four hotels and guest houses accommodate visitors during the mid-May to Columbus Day season. Camping is not allowed.

The island has an interesting history. Its fishing banks were worked by European maritime powers as early as 1500. During the 1600s, Monhegan was the site of several short-lived attempts at settlement, with control of the island contested by both the French and the British. A pirates' base of operation in the early 1700s, Monhegan may have been visited by Viking ships around the year 1100.

Present-day Monhegan will be a disappointment to anyone looking for cute boutiques and nightlife. Blissful quiet (except for a foghorn) and a sense of slowing down, reducing one's pace, are to be expected on Monhegan. Besides its cottages and few hotels, the village boasts two shops (island maps sold), a chapel, and a little schoolhouse and library. Physically, the island is shaped like a giant granite whaleback. Its cliffs plunge abruptly to the sea, especially on the Atlantic side. A hill caps Monhegan's west-central section, atop which sits Monhegan Light. The built-up area of the island and its dock rest in a hollow below and to the west of the light, opposite Manana. The village's one gravel road, with its several spurs, runs roughly north and south from the rise above the dock.

Although you can make a day trip to Monhegan in summer, you're strongly advised to stay at least overnight, and 3 days make an ideal visit. *Be sure to have advance reservations.* For more information on Monhegan Boat schedules and accommodations, call the Maine Tourism Association at 1-888-624-6345 or the Monhegan Boat Line at 207-372-8848.

A visit to Monhegan should take into account the very fragile ecology of the island and the reality that in high summer this island is often overcrowded with zealous day-trippers. This puts tremendous pressure on Monhegan's facilities and limited freshwater supply, to say nothing of spoiling the tranquil, remote peacefulness that is synonymous with Monhegan life. The advent of extra boat trips to the island in recent summers has increased the severity of this problem. Does this mean hiking Monhegan is out? No. I strongly urge you to make your journey in May or September and October, when the island is usually uncrowded and serene, and when accommodations are usually cheaper.

Use great caution with fire on Monhegan. Smoking is not allowed anywhere on the island outside of the immediate village area. Campfires are prohibited in all parts of the island. Trailbikes are not permitted on the island trails. Please be sure to carry away what you bring onto the island.

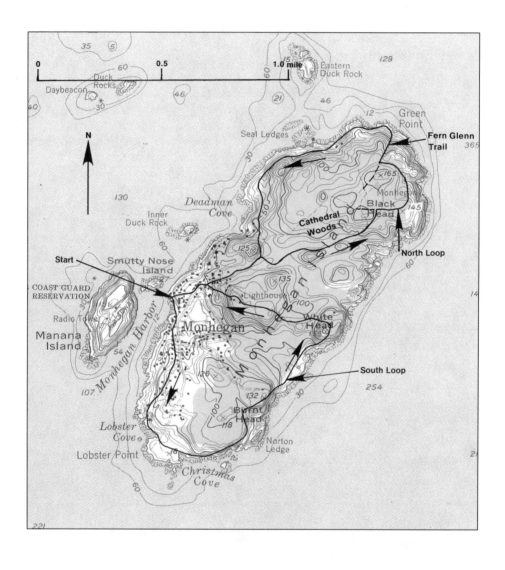

16

Monhegan South Loop

Distance (around loop): 2 miles

Hiking time: 1½ hours

Vertical rise: 50 feet

Map: USGS 7½' Monhegan

Nearly 20 trails link various parts of Monhegan, but there are two major loop walks on the island that include most of its spectacular scenery. The longer of these two loops makes a broad circuit of the southern end of the island and takes you by Lobster Cove, Christmas Cove, Burnt Head, and White Head.

To begin the south-island loop, start at the Monhegan Church. Walk south through the village, past the Monhegan House, and up the hill. Meandering by several houses, the gravel road continues southward, gradually running out into a grassy Jeep track. The track ends above the rocky ex-

Monhegan Village and Harbor

panse of Lobster Cove, where there are good views west toward the distant mainland. At this point, a pathway, sometimes hard to find, continues eastward through the open, thick swale. To the south lies the small ledge known as the Washerwoman, and, ahead, a similar rock rib called Norton Ledge. Watch for the rusty wreck of the Sheridan thrust up on the rocks here.

Following the edge of the land, you shortly turn northeast and north, passing Gull Rock. The trail climbs slightly, moving in and out of mixed spruce and balsam growth and over weathered ledge. The Underhill and Burnt Head Trails are passed on your left as you approach and cross Burnt Head.

Continuing along the shoreline, the route next bends to your right around Gull Cove to 160-foot White Head, one of the two highest points on the island's seaward perimeter. The views are exceptional here, and there are a number of spots to stretch out and relax on the grass.

The White Head Trail, a path which becomes a grassy tote road, leaves the head and runs nearly due west. Follow this road toward the village, and you'll soon pass a sports field on your left near the center of the island and the power station. Moments later, still walking west, you'll arrive at Monhegan Light. The lighthouse is a pretty edifice, and attached to it you'll find a small museum replete with exhibits on the island's natural and social history. Excellent views of Manana (now uninhabited) and the mainland are yours from the lighthouse lawn.

Continue westward on the now rather rocky road, which winds quickly down to a junction by the schoolhouse. Keep left here, and you'll come, in a few minutes, to your starting point on "Main Street." Although this route can easily be walked in 1½ hours, so pleasant is it on a fair day that you may want to allow several hours and pack food and water along.

17

Monhegan North Loop

Distance (around loop): 1¾ miles

Hiking time: 1½ hours

Vertical rise: 100 feet

Map: USGS 7½' Monhegan

The loop around Monhegan's northern reaches provides an interesting hill-and-dale route through a landscape that is somewhat different from but just as attractive as the island's southern perimeter. This walk takes you through Monhegan's beautiful Cathedral Woods section and thence out onto the northern cliffs and rocks. Although this route can be walked in one and a half hours, the spectacular views and serene wooded areas will probably demand more of your time, and a leisurely walk of two to three hours makes a more reasonable schedule.

The Monhegan North Loop begins in front of the Monhegan Gallery, above the dock. From this point, head northeast on the gravel road past the schoolhouse. In about ¼ mile, the Cathedral Woods Trail (Number 11) is located on your right. Enter the woods here, proceeding eastward. The trail follows the north end of a kidney-shaped marsh to your right. Momentarily, you walk through Cathedral Woods, one of the most attractive spots on the island. The woods make a quiet sanctuary of tall red spruce, balsam, and pine. The trail is carpeted with the fallen needles of these coniferous trees.

Your chances of coming across deer are excellent in this quiet, wooded part of the island. Many deer paths intersect the main trails of the island and are often mistaken for the trails. The deer paths are narrow and brush-choked, and they often end abruptly on a ledge, leaving you stranded. Stick to the marked pathways.

The trail next swings to the north as it

A fishing shack on Monhegan Island

nears Black Head and connects with the Black Head Trail (west) and the Cliff Trail (east). Turn right at this junction, following the Cliff Trail northward through the woods and along the headlands past Black Head and above Pulpit Rock. The route soon passes a junction with the Station Hill Trail, where you keep right, continuing above the water. Swinging westward, the more inland, you reach a T, where you bear right on the Fern Glenn Trail (Number 17) and walk north to Green Point on Monhegan's north shore. This is the northernmost outcrop on the island. Turning west, it's only a short distance to Pebbly Beach. There are excellent views offshore to where Eastern Duck Island looms to the north, with Seal Ledges in the foreground.

Passing another trail on your left, proceed southwesterly along the shoreline, around Calf Cove. Nigh Duck and Smutty Nose Islands may be seen here, lying farther to the southwest on a line with Manana. There are also good views of the mainland for the leisurely walker along these bluffs.

The trail moves away from Calf Cove and Deadman's Cove, turning now to the east and south. Your route connects with the Pebbly Beach Trail, where you keep right, turning south and shortly reaching the gravel road. Walk right on the road, pass the tiny schoolhouse again, and arrive in a few minutes at your starting point in the village.

Note: Climbing around the great sea cliffs of Monhegan's eastern headlands is a tempting pastime. However, the possibility of dangerous falls into the sea is always present, and given strong currents, isolation, and undertows, rescue would be unlikely. Hikers visiting the island are urged to stick to the regular, marked trails for their own safety. Parents should use caution in monitoring the activities of children in this area.

IV

Central Region and Oxford Hills

18

Monument Hill

Distance (round trip): 1½ miles

Hiking time: 1 hour

Vertical rise: 300 feet

Map: USGS 7½' Pico Peak

Rising to the west over Androscoggin Lake in Leeds, Monument Hill is a low, drumlin-shaped mountain that affords an easy hike for individuals or families, yet offers some majestic views westward over wooded central Maine to the White Mountains of New Hampshire. Roughly 16 miles southwest and west of the state capital, Monument Hill lies in the rolling farm country of south-central Maine in an area riddled with lakes, ponds, and streams. This attractive hill is a highly visible landmark from nearby country roads and can be seen on the approach.

To reach the mountain, take US 202 to its midpoint between Lewiston and Augusta, a bit northeast of Greene. Turn north on ME 106 and drive just over 6 miles to Leeds. Passing a store on your right in Leeds center, make an immediate left off ME 106 and up Church Hill Road. Follow Church Hill Road as it rises gradually westward and watch for the community medical center on your left. Just beyond the medical center, turn right on North Road. Continue to the trailhead about 1 mile north of this junction. A sign and several large boulders mark the trailhead. Roadside parking is available on the shoulder.

The route up Monument Hill has been modified recently. Some good trail work now makes it possible to hike a pleasant loop over the mountain, returning to your starting point without retracing your steps. Begin by the boulders underneath the attractive sprawl of some great oaks bordered by a grove of beeches. A grassy woods road dotted with raspberry patches

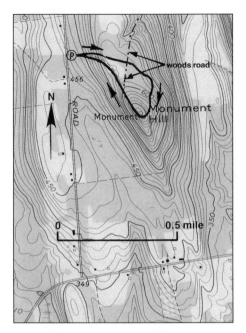

runs eastward and immediately passes another road that comes in from the right. Walking past this side road (follow arrow on tree), continue east into a stand of hemlocks where the trail pulls southeast.

The path now becomes more stony and rises steadily in beech, hemlock, and silver birch. The walk continues around to the northeast, enters a cluster of pines, and soon levels off. The trail is marked by prominent gray blazes here. You next walk southeast through a corridor of low brush, past the remains of an apple orchard, and through further pretty stands of pine and birch. About ½ mile into the woods, pass a grassy road marked by a pile of stones on your right and continue southeast.

The road bends south through fragrant pines and balsams with thick ranges of ferns on both sides. Arching right, left, and right again, the path runs up a slight grade bordered by oak, maple, and white birch. A series of exposed, gray granite ledges lies to the right. Shortly, you enter a clearing where, in any season but high summer, there are partial views eastward over Androscoggin Lake. The trail now pulls sharply right and runs up a short grade to the tall stone plinth, a Civil War monument.

Monument Hill's views are primarily to the west. Indeed, as noted earlier, they range from the nearby rolling hills of central Maine all the way into New Hampshire, where the Carter-Moriah Range and the Presidentials can be seen on the distant horizon. Maine's Mahoosuc Range lies to the west-northwest. More northerly is cone-shaped Mount Blue over Weld and, much farther north, the four peaks of the great, east–west mass of Bigelow Mountain. In winter, with the trees bare, Mount Pisgah in Winthrop and Monmouth may be seen to the southeast. When more temperate weather prevails in July and August, patches of low-bush blueberries bloom around the summit, and you can easily spend a few warm summer hours here enjoying the splendid outlook to the west.

To continue the loop and return to North Road, follow the grassy tote road north and northwest off the summit. Mixed-growth woods, more blueberries, and ground juniper border the trail. Strips of granite ledge protrude through the grass underfoot. As the road descends, young black oaks are seen, and some limited views to the northwest occur. Gray blazes on the ledge outcrops mark the way as the trail climbs down quickly into some handsome deciduous cover. Enter a canopy of hardwoods and pass a road to your right as you continue downhill (left) in the direction of the arrow on a nearby tree.

Here and there the protesting chatter of red squirrels sounds in the trees. The road widens, dropping through stands of balsam, pine, and white birch. The familiar patter of black-capped chickadees and the plaintive peeping note of circling nut-hatches are often heard. You soon pass the blasted skeleton of an old tree, and the trail bends left, then right, entering a corridor of superb old white pines where the air is pleasingly fragrant. Descending farther through a low, grassy spot, you cross several log walks. In a couple of minutes, come to the junction with the main trail and turn left (west), arriving shortly at North Road.

Because this loop over Monument Hill is seldom very steep, it is an excellent snowshoe route or cross-country ski trip in winter. You should be prepared, however, for heady winds out of the northwest on the summit in the colder months.

19

Mount Philip

Distance (round trip): 1 mile

Hiking time: 45 minutes

Vertical rise: 300 feet

Map: USGS 7½' Belgrade Lakes

More than once, a friend who lives in Maine's Belgrade Lakes region had urged me to sample the smaller peaks that ring these attractive lakes and ponds. One day I took him up on the invitation, and the ramble through these hills was a salutary one. Of the several good walks in this neighborhood, I think the easy hike up Mount Philip is the most satisfying, and it is described here. This walk is a gradual, undemanding ascent up accommodating grades to a summit with excellent views and makes an ideal outing for families with youngsters.

The Belgrade Lakes region has been one of Maine's grand summer destinations for over a century. Centered on the little towns of Belgrade, Rome, and Oakland, the area includes five major bodies of water and eight to ten smaller ponds. Long Pond and Great Pond in Belgrade, North Pond and East Pond in Rome, and Snow Pond (Messalonskee) in Belgrade and Oakland are the larger waters at the hub of the area. Ward, Salmon, McGrath, Whittier, and Watson Ponds lie scattered over the region. There are others. The area has not been heavily developed, as many lakes regions often become, and though many camps dot the shores, these villages and outlands—less than 20 miles north of Augusta, the state capitol—remain wooded, rural, and quiet.

Mount Philip, named for Philip Snow, an early settler here, is approached on ME 27 from Augusta and Belgrade, or alternatively via ME 137 and ME 225 from Waterville. Coming from the east, you'll spot the trailhead a mile west of the Rome Country

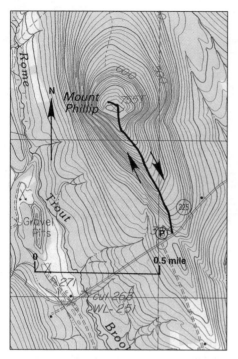

siderably more open feel in late fall, winter, and early spring.

You'll pass some tall white birches and several old hemlocks picked apart by porcupines. You cannot help but notice that, despite clusters of hemlock and spruce, these woods are mainly second-growth hardwoods, the area probably being last cut over 40 or 50 years ago. The gentle terrain, bits of granite visible here and there, and leafy ground cover all make for very attractive walking as you meander north and northwest. Starflowers and bluets grow along the path in places.

In ¼ mile, the trail pulls slightly more to the northwest and climbs a bit more steadily. On my most recent walk here, an adult osprey *(Pandion haliaetus)* circled above, howling in protest, as I was apparently too close to a nest somewhere nearby. Ospreys are making a comeback in Maine, and they like to build their giant twig nests in tall, forked trees within short flying distance of ponds or streams where the fishing is handy. This bird had built a nest uncomfortably close to a trail frequented by humans and tried to drive me off both coming and going, uttering cries of alarm.

The trail next passes the beginning of some oak cover and enters a grove of old white pines, typically 60 or 70 feet high. Farther on, some very young beech and ash form a canopy over the trail, beyond which you move into a more open area dotted with young oaks. Just under ½ mile from the road, a series of granite ledges lies ahead. The route ascends these ledges directly on a short series of switchbacks. The trail now bears left and, amid stands of more white oaks, meanders westward for a short distance along the top of the ledges and reaches its high point.

Views to the south over Great Pond and

Store on ME 225. Or, from the junction of ME 27 and ME 225 north of Belgrade, drive east and reach the trailhead 1.1 miles east of the Rome Community Center. The trail's entry to the woods is marked only by a yellow sign indicating a bend in the road. The trail enters the woods on the *north* side of ME 225 here. Since there's no safe parking at this spot, leave your car at a gravel turnout a couple hundred yards *west* of the trailhead near Central Maine Power (CMP) pole 25–also on the north side of ME 225– and walk to the trail.

The walk begins with a scramble up a bank by the sign, and, walking to the north, you quickly enter dense, deciduous woods. The entire trail is obvious to the eye, and, though not recently marked, is easily followed. Beech, ash, scattered maple, and hemlock border the path as it runs along very gentle grades. This route is heavily shaded and cool in summer, but has a con-

Central Maine lakes

to the hills to the southwest and west are found here. The summit ledge is a good place to hold a picnic and to enjoy the scenery for a while. It's also possible to scout the wooded country behind the summit. In the months when the leaves are gone, some views to the northwest and west can be discovered. (This low summit has become increasingly brushy. You may have to move about to gain outlooks on distant lakes and mountains.) When you're ready to descend, simply retrace your steps carefully to the road.

With the exception of the brief rise to the summit ledges, grades are very easy on this walk and snowshoeing or Nordic skiing the route in winter is quite possible. Given its mainly hardwood cover, the walk up Mount Philip is spectacularly colorful (as are the views) in autumn.

20

Black Mountain

Distance (round trip): 3½ miles

Hiking time: 2½ hours

Vertical rise: 1,250 feet

Map: USGS 7½' Worthley Pond

Sumner is one of those nice little backwoods towns in the foothills of the western Maine Mountains where the flavor of a Maine that is fast disappearing still exists. And, on a dead-end road in farm country here, you'll find Black Mountain, an inviting, low summit in the midst of the Oxford Hills. Black Mountain is sufficiently remote that you're likely to have it to yourself on most any day of the week.

To find the trail, drive along ME 219 from either east or west, and watch for its junction with a side road that runs north to Peru a couple of miles east of West Sumner. This road is just under 4 miles west of the junction of ME 219 and ME 140. Turn north on this side road and drive 1.5 miles to a fork dominated by an old white schoolhouse with a flagpole. Bear left (northwest) on Black Mountain Road. This road forks in about 0.75 mile; you keep right at the fork and follow the road to the trailhead on your left just before the road ends at a farmhouse. Park on the shoulder on the west side of the road by a yellow marker. Please be careful not to block either road.

Your walk begins on a logging road that heads west and northwest through grown-up farmland laced with blackberry bushes. Stone walls border the trail. In summer, this brushy terrain is alive with many bird species. Here I once saw my first scarlet tanager in years. About ⅓ mile from your starting point, turn right where a less-used road enters the woods toward an old lumbering site. This road, no more than a rutted track, crosses a tiny, seasonal brook and pulls briefly right (north) before emerging into a

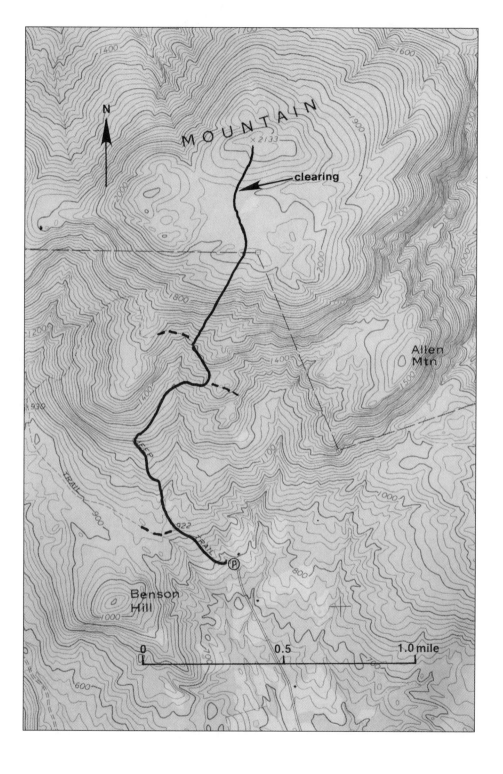

Pink lady's slippers, an increasingly rare flower in Maine

clearing. The road is often damp here under the shady canopy. Watch carefully now for a small cairn in front of a clump of trees. Bear left (northwest), crossing a stream and following another grassy woods road at this cairn. You're in pretty, deciduous growth here, the trail bordered with beech, birch, maple, and oak as you walk. The stream is now on your right.

The route climbs steadily northwest and the disused logging road you're on gradually narrows and becomes more grassy and grown up. As the route pulls away from the brook, ascend a ridge, then turn more eastward, slabbing this same rise and gaining altitude steadily. Views back to the southwest begin to open up.

Ground cover is varied, including clintonia lilies, blackberries, sarsaparilla, mea-dow rue, self-heal, cinquefoil, bluets, wild oats, and violets. At ¾ mile, the route levels off and pulls around to your right (east), soon crossing a brook bed, and then resumes its ascent. By any stretch of the imagination, you're in bear country and you may see tracks in soft ground.

The trail now narrows further, becoming a rocky path that is itself a streambed during spring runoff. The woods begin to undergo a transformation here, becoming coniferous, with increasing stands of red spruce and balsam. The trail passes through several groves of spruce, which grow in tightly along the trail, creating a low canopy in places.

A little over 1 mile from where you parked, the grassy path levels off at a height-of-land. *Look for another cairn here* where you turn left onto an even less distinct tote road to the north and northwest. Layers of naked granite outcrops begin to appear on your right as you follow this new road a few hundred yards upward. Keep your eyes open for another cairn and some logs that shortly direct you *off* this tote road to your right and onto the path to the summit.

The summit path now gains altitude quickly, following a seasonal brook upward to the east and northeast. The path crosses and recrosses the brook several times, rising steadily. The character of the mountain has changed completely here, with nearly all hardwood cover gone and dense clusters of softwoods taking over. You'll often see the beautiful shape and color of painted trillium along the trail. Canada mayflower, bunchberries, and low-bush blueberries are also found as you ascend. Much of the elevation gained on this hike occurs in this section, as you zig-zag upward over hard-packed sphagnum moss and encounter another seasonal brook.

You wind shortly through sparse fir, spruce, and birch and reach a clearing dotted with sheep laurel, a flash of bright pink in midsummer. Follow the cairns over the ledges and through beautiful clumps of lady's slippers, which are in bloom from early to mid-June. About 1¾ miles from the trailhead, you arrive at the open ledges just below Black's wooded, 2,100-foot summit.

The ledge is composed of the pegmatite so common in western Maine. Veins of quartz bisect the granite, and reindeer lichen shaded by fine spruce is in evidence. The views range from northeast to south here. Tumbledown Dick is seen over Mud Pond. To the east, you'll spot Ragged Jack and The Saddleback. Around in the south are Labrador Pond and the Nezinscot River valley.

Black Mountain may be worth several trips in various seasons. A hike just to see the lady's slippers (which are protected and should not be picked) is in order. The mountain's fine, panoramic views are equally enjoyable in foliage season, late September and early October. Except for the brief sections where grades are prominent, the mountain can be snowshoed as well.

Returning to your car, be careful not to miss the turns on and off the old logging road at the midpoint of the walk. Since there are no springs on this trail, it's wise to carry some drinking water, whatever the season.

21

Bald Mountain (Woodstock) and Speckled Mountain (West Peru)

Distance (round trip): 4 miles

Hiking time: 3 hours

Vertical rise: 1,500 feet

Map: USGS 7½' Mount Zircon

For the boastful hiker who'd like to claim two distinct summits in a single outing, this walk will do nicely. The route described here takes in the summits of two beautiful, pillarlike mountains that rise in the midst of three remote ponds in west-central Maine. That this outing lies in backcountry far from the madding highway makes for just that much more frosting on the cake. A relatively short hike (4 miles), this circuit nonetheless involves some steep sections that provide the feeling of the bigger hills to the north, and the superb, panoramic views simply enhance this impression.

Bald and Speckled Mountains are reached by traveling ME 219 east or west to the town of East Sumner and turning north on a side road 3.3 miles west of the elementary school. Follow this side road for about 1.5 miles, then go left (west) on Labrador Pond Road—which runs along the south end of this pretty body of water, with its fine views of nearby mountains. You shortly join another road that comes in on your left, and continue north, bearing left on Black Mountain Road at an old schoolhouse now converted into a dwelling. Leave Black Mountain Road just under 2.5 miles from the schoolhouse to go left on Redding Road. From this junction, drive 4.9 miles to Shagg Pond. At the tiny public landing, you'll have excellent views across the pond of both of the mountains you'll hike. Drive 0.5 mile beyond Shagg Pond and up the hill on an increasingly rough road. Near the top of the incline, you'll find on your left a gravel space big enough for several cars. Park here opposite a sign reading FIRE LANE 1010.

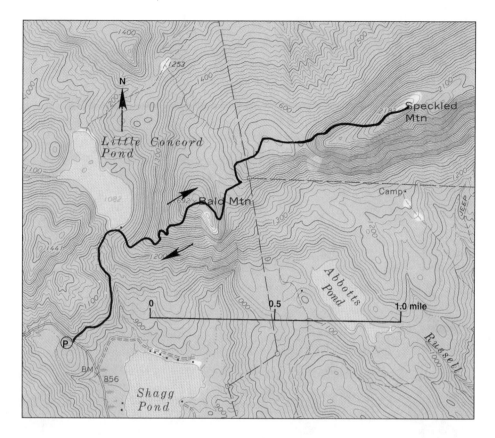

Begin your walk by heading southeast and east on the gravel fire lane under a tall canopy of beeches. The terrain here is attractive, particularly in autumn when through the trees there are glimpses of Shagg Pond. Dropping gradually to the east, the road pulls around to the north over a seasonal brook and through a grove of hemlocks before crossing a rib of exposed ledge. Passing a rocky overhang on your right, the route drops farther into a slump and divides into three tracks, any one of which will take you over the next rise, where the tracks merge into one again. The path now continues along the wide fire lane to the northeast and north, arriving after ⅔ mile at Little Concord Pond.

Just before you reach the shore of this attractive pond, bear right on a blue-blazed trail and climb directly up a ledge to your right. Under hemlock and red spruce, the route climbs briskly east and southeast on exposed ledge sprinkled with mica schist and quartzite. Views to the west and south soon begin to open up. The trail meanders eastward while rising steadily, passes a downed birch, and plateaus briefly, offering more views over Shagg Pond and the hills to the west. Tall white pines and hemlocks provide cover over this narrow, eastward-trending rib of land as you walk upward. Some old pines in this section have been reduced to ruins by pileated woodpeckers searching for insects in their trunks.

The trail next moves through a stand of

Speckled Mountain from the summit of Bald Mountain

red oak and birch, where views to the north open up occasionally. Meandering still upward toward the east, the trail soon crests on the summit ledges of Bald. There must be an acre of open ledge here, with spectacular views to the ranges immediately west and southwest. Shagg Pond provides a mirrorlike surface far below. On a sunny day, it's so pleasant here that you'll just want to sit, eat lunch, and enjoy the grand perspective ranging from southeast to northwest.

When you're ready to take in your second peak of the day, follow the ledges through clumps of rhodora to the southeast and east, watching for blue blazes. You'll enjoy an excellent view of Speckled Mountain here just before you reenter hemlock and spruce woods and descend steeply to the northeast. Drop into stands of beech on a boulder-strewn col between the two mountains where fine views southward toward pretty Abbott Pond occur. Crossing a seasonal brook and a snowmobile trail, continue east-northeast on level ground and enter spruce woods again on the blue-blazed trail, shortly passing a low stone plinth marked "1916."

Now continue north-northeastward through alternating open, ledgy clearings and shady corridors of spruce. Cairns or boulders mark the clearings. Clumps of chalk green lichen, borders of haircap moss, and lowbush blueberries line the shaded trail. You soon pull east in a corridor of black birch at the top of the col and walk directly east to the steep west face of Speckled Mountain. Here your work begins again.

The trail now heads right up Speckled, where good outlooks to the northwest are seen. The grades are continuously steep for a short distance, and then the route moves under the west ledges of Speckled, turns south, and climbs quickly onto those ledges. Dikes of quartzite and deposits of mica schist and feldspar glint in the granitic rock. Magnificent views to the northwest and west are yours here. The tree-studded ridge of Bald Mountain lies immediately back to the west.

The route now slabs along the north side of the ridge, rising steadily through low spruce and passing through a series of open ledges with domelike formations. Broad outlooks to the south open up through the trees. In a few more minutes, you emerge on the summit ledges marked by an old US Geodetic Survey seal and the figures "2207" carved in the rock.

The scene here deserves the term *spectacular,* with views in nearly all directions. The white-topped mountain to the west of Rumford's Mills is Rumford Whitecap (see Hike 22). Black Mountain stands nearby to the east. Sunday River Whitecap, Old Speck, and Baldpate are far to the northwest. The distinctive east–west profile of Saddleback looms well to the north, and to its east lies Mount Abraham. On a clear day, Mount Washington and the northern Presidentials can be spotted on the western horizon. There are, in fact, too many mountains visible from here to be listed easily. On a bright day, you can count perhaps 40 summits of varying elevation around the horizon, giving you the feeling that Speckled is more lofty than its modest 2,200 feet would suggest.

When you're reluctantly prepared to leave this attractive summit, retrace your steps west to Bald Mountain, watching for the familiar blue blazes all the way to Little Concord Pond and thence out the fire road to where you parked.

The trail described here is currently well maintained by Roger and Laurie Doran.

22

Rumford Whitecap

Distance (round trip): 4 miles

Hiking time: 2½ hours

Vertical rise: 1,550 feet

Map: USGS 7½' East Andover

A grand walk in the sturdy, unspoiled hill country of western Maine, the hike up Rumford Whitecap offers first-class views all over its surrounding region and well into New Hampshire. Not far northwest of the paper-mill town of Rumford, this rangy, bare-crested mountain isn't heavily used, and a hike here provides rich rewards for very modest exertion. The windswept, light-colored, granitic ledges that give the mountain its name allow open-ridge walking usually found only on higher, more arduous peaks.

From east or west, approach the mountain via US 2, where, just west of Rumford Point, you bear north on ME 5 in the direction of Andover. Three miles above US 2, turn right and cross the Ellis River. Almost immediately, in 0.25 mile, bear left (north) on a paved road and follow it for 1.7 miles. When you reach Coburn Brook Road, go right. Stay on this road as it meanders past a farm for 0.7 mile to a clearing on your right between two houses. Park off the road opposite a telephone pole marked "16/16." A small footbridge that crosses Coburn Brook also lies opposite.

Once under way, you'll find that the early section of the trail loses no time rising steeply to the southeast and east on a gravel logging road. Moose frequent this quiet neighborhood, and you're likely to see in the path some very large tracks of the great animals. The route follows a broad cut eastward, passing a tote road that drops into a brushy defile and crosses a brook to your right. Tall white pines, hemlock, and red spruce line the road. Pass a

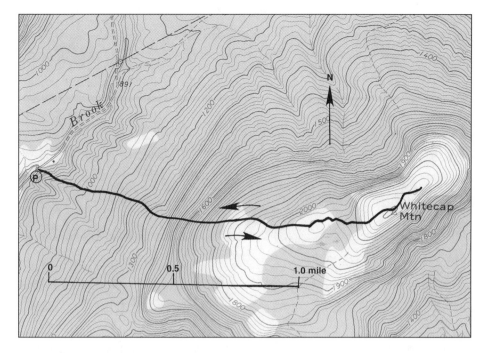

stone wall that angles off toward the south, and follow the trail as it moves around to the south-southeast, going over several gravel water bars.

Climbing steadily southeastward, pass old stone cellar holes on both sides of the road, and arrive at a fork just as you enter a grassy, unused yarding area. Keeping to the right, cross the yard and swing steeply uphill to the south as the road heads toward the summit. You continue to rise amid tall pines in terrain littered in some places with slash. Pass a road leading off to the southwest and continue southeastward. A second fork is reached and you keep left, eventually running east and east-northeast on a rougher surface. Soon, climbing into terrain dotted with hardwoods, cross two small brooks that travel down off the mountain at gravel water bars.

Just beyond the *second* brook and ⅔ mile from where you parked, watch for two small stone cairns to the right of the road. The trail leaves the road here and runs westward for a short distance into a rough, cutover, hardwood clearing. About 50 yards in from the gravel right-of-way, the trail abruptly pulls left uphill out of the clearing and begins its brisk, southeasterly ascent to the summit ledges.

Though not marked, the footpath is clear from here on. Continue to rise steadily southeast and east in maple, spruce, and beech cover. A slash-filled right-of-way parallels the trail to your right for a short distance. Soon you arrive at the beginning of the ledges, rising onto open, moss-covered rock. The first open views back to the west and northwest occur in this section. The trail then meanders generally eastward over open ledge bordered by forested land. A series of small cairns marks the way. Views back to the west and northwest get better and better as you ascend. Gradually, fine outlooks northeastward and north open up, as do panoramic views southwest toward New Hampshire's Presidentials.

Continuing eastward, pass through two

The view west from Rumford Whitecap

islands of spruce cover and crest the highest point on the ridge. It's a walk of only another 100 yards to the end of the ridge and the east summit, with its excellent views to surrounding hills, Rumford, and Andover. To the immediate north, a perfect bowl of a valley exists, surrounded by mountains on all sides. Mostly invisible, the US Navy's worldwide satellite communications antenna system nestles in this quiet, sparsely settled valley, formerly communicating with—among others—the submerged submarine fleet.

Except for the odd clump of spruce growth on the summit ledges, you can see in all directions on this last section of ridge, and the scene is magnificent. Antenna-capped Black Mountain stands close to eastward. Rolling hills and farmhouses form the immediate landscape to the southwest. On clear days, Mount Washington, New England's highest summit, is visible on the far southwestern horizon. Tumble-

down Mountain and the distinctive cone shape of Mount Blue lie well off to the north-northeast.

When you leave the summit, retrace your steps to your car, being careful to stay on the main right-of-way as you descend into the woods, avoiding side roads.

Note: Hikers should carry a compass and the map provided here on this walk. The path, which follows the main gravel logging road on the west side of the mountain, is only marked on the summit ridge. Many side roads, cutovers, and junctions intersect the main trail. Logging activity may create new avenues. Route-finding with your compass may be necessary occasionally. A partial relocation of the trail on the ridge is being discussed at present. Watch carefully for possible departures from the trail description included here.

V

Evans Notch Region

23

Deer Hill

Distance (round trip): 4 miles

Hiking time: 2 hours

Vertical rise: 1250 feet

*Maps: USGS 7½' Center Lovell, Maine;
USGS 15' North Conway, New
Hampshire; Chatham Trails Association
Map of CTA Service Area*

Big Deer and Little Deer are the two interesting summits of a rise known as Deer Hill in the midst of the intervale below Evans Notch. Two gem mines are found on the mountain, as is a reliable limestone spring that furnishes very potable, cool water. Although a low mountain, Deer makes a fine lookout for examining the hills of the Evans Notch area and the high peaks of the White Mountains to the west. Perhaps best of all, Deer Hill is set back in the woods off secluded ME 113, far from the traffic and noise of more developed tourist regions. When you want a quiet day in pretty countryside, try this route.

The loop around the two summits of Deer Hill is reached from either north or south on ME 113. If approaching from the north, turn south on 113 by the Wild River in Gilead. If coming from the south, drive north on 113 from the village center in Fryeburg. Turn east by a bridge over Chandler Brook approximately 13.5 miles south of Gilead or 1.75 miles north of the junction of 113 and the north end of the loop road to Chatham center. The dirt road onto which you turn crosses Chandler Brook about 0.3 mile in from the pavement. This turn is 0.5 mile south of the AMC Cold River Camp. The AMC site makes a good point during the summer months to inquire if you need directions or information on local trails. You may purchase a copy of the invaluable CTA local map here, too.

Drive east on the graded forest service road, passing a small tarn. Beyond several fields on your right, you will come, in a little less than 1 mile, to a prominent sign on

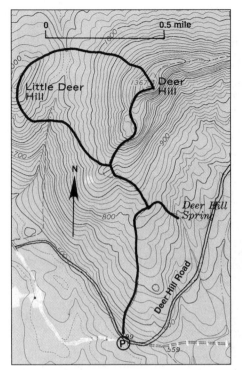

trail here runs north along the tote road to one of the old mine sites and may be explored if you wish to add extra time and distance to the basic route described here.) You reach a junction on a knoll about ¾ miles from the spot where you parked.

Stay with the yellow blazes as you walk through old maples, beech, birch, and tall oaks. This more open woodland reveals wintergreen and spinulose woodfern scattered along the ground.

Shortly you ascend a ridge and emerge via bare ledges on an open knoll. The stony path here is comprised of pegmatitic granite, rich with quartz, mica, and feldspar deposits. Amethysts lie hidden and embedded in this once molten rock. Here on the sheer south slope of Big Deer there are good views to the White Mountains of New Hampshire, east to Harndon Hill, and over Little Deer to the immediate west.

Cairns and more yellow blazes direct you over ledge and through woods to another lookout over Big Deer's southeast flanks. Wild blueberries and clusters of trailing arbutus line the path. A beaver bog lies off to the east of the trail. A small mine to the north yields amethyst, feldspar, garnet, muscovite, and pyrite. Across to the southeast are Harndon, Lord, and Pine Hills (see Hike 24). You can make out the long curve of Horseshoe Pond to the east of Lord Hill.

From this ledge, walk up through bracken, fern, sheep laurel, and lady's slippers (protected) to the 1,367-foot summit of Big Deer. Through the trees, the striking form of Baldface becomes visible across the valley. The trail now dips westward along the col to Little Deer. After some steep drops to the west and northwest, the route levels off in oak, beech, and hemlock growth and works uphill again to Little Deer after a steep stretch. Baldface, across ME 113, now can be seen clearly in all its rangy

your left on a banking that marks the trail to Deer Hill Spring. The spring, which is the source of Colton Brook, lies on your way to Big Deer summit. Leave the road here and head north into the woods, following the yellow-blazed trail up what once served as a mining road. Tall red pines and white birch border the route. You head uphill on easy grades for about ⅓ mile, leveling off shortly in groves of white pine, birch, and maple. Continue on this disused road, being careful not to turn onto any of the several side trails.

A bit more than ½ mile into the woods, watch for the trail to Deer Hill Spring. Take a moment to make the short side trip to the spring by turning right here. Water in this unusually large spring is filtered through a vein of limestone, rendering it milky but very good to drink. Back at the junction, follow a trail northwest toward Big Deer. (Another

Deer Hill

magnificence. You'll also see more of the familiar pegmatite here as this summit, like the
others nearby, is part of the same metamor-
phic rock mass.

Two trails lead off Little Deer's summit.
The one to the northwest goes to the AMC
Cold River Camp mentioned earlier. Take the
left trail, which runs south, and enter the red
pines and black spruce, descending toward
the forest service road once again. Pass to
the left of the Ledges Trail, following the
cairns down the open ledges. Soon you

come to a trail junction. The route to your left
runs east toward Big Deer, passing an abandoned mica and feldspar mine. Keep *left* here
and walk southeast and east, descending
gradually. This path carries you back, in about
a mile, to the trail junction you passed earlier
above the spring. Continue to this junction,
and descend southeastward toward the
spring, the side trail to which you pass shortly.
Bearing southwest and south, continue your
descent, arriving soon at the gravel road and
parking area.

24

The Conant Trail: Pine Hill, Lord Hill, Harndon Hill

Distance (round trip): 5½ miles

Hiking time: 4 hours

Vertical rise: 1,200 feet

Maps: USGS 7½' Center Lovell, Maine; USGS 15' North Conway, New Hampshire; Chatham Trails Association Map of CTA Service Area

The Conant Trail in Stow forms an elongated circuit over two 1,200-foot-plus mountains in the border country of western Maine. Like its neighbors, Big and Little Deer Mountains (see Hike 23), the Conant Trail lies at the south end of Evans Notch off a Maine road that meanders in and out of New Hampshire. At the most easterly point on the Conant Trail, there are some unique geological resources and striking views of beautiful Horseshoe Pond. This ramble through the unspoiled backcountry of the Cold River region makes a perfect day hike of moderate length.

The Conant Trail can be approached from east or west. From the west, drive south from Gilead or north from Fryeburg on ME 113. Turn east on a gravel road at a bridge over Chandler Brook. This bridge is 13.5 miles south of Gilead. Alternatively, it's 1.75 miles north of the junction of the north end of Chatham Loop Road and ME 113; or 0.5 mile south of the AMC Cold River Camp. The trailhead is 1.5 miles east of the point where you leave ME 113 in Stow.

From the east, you can approach the trailhead by taking gravel Deer Hill Road west from near the inn buildings at Evergreen Valley in North Lovell, Maine, off ME 5. The trailhead is 4.8 miles west of the point where you hit the gravel road at Evergreen Valley.

Coming from either direction, turn south at a big white pine with a small CTA CHATHAM TRAILS ASSOCIATION sign and drive in 50 yards from Deer Hill Road. Where another woods road comes in from your right, park out of the way on the grassy shoulder.

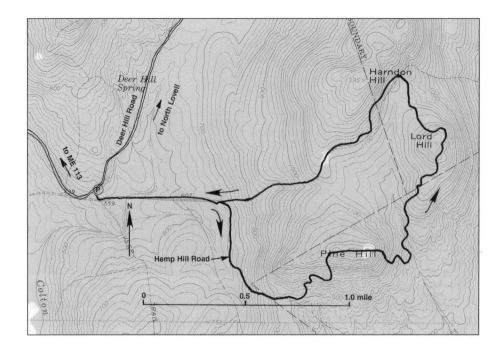

With some water and perhaps lunch in your rucksack, follow a woods road to the left (east), passing through a clearing and over a causeway that bisects Colton Brook deadwater. A dam lies up to your right. Continue east and southeast on this stoney gravel road, rising in beech, hemlock, red pine, and birch. You soon pass a small A-frame camp on your right and a stone house on your left. There are lovely, brushy stone walls on both sides of the road. You'll pass several grassy turnouts before the trail turns right (south) on another gravel track, known as Hemp Hill Road. This point marks the beginning and end of a circuit, roughly 5 miles in length, over Pine, Lord, and Harndon Hills. Watch for yellow blazes marking this turn. Wild sarsaparilla and bracken fern line Hemp Hill Road, along which you now walk to the south and southeast, rising gradually. Dip into a hollow, crossing a corrugated bridge over a small, seasonal brook, and, reentering national

forest land, pass by a cutover area to your right. Through the trees to your left are occasional good views of the impressive hanging cliffs on the west side of Pine Hill. The road narrows as it continues to rise southward through mature hemlock, oak, and spruce.

Roughly ¾ mile from where you parked, watch for the old cellar holes of the long-abandoned Johnson farm, and bear immediately left as the trail leaves Hemp Hill Road. Passing another CTA sign, the path now climbs noticeably to the northeast in white pine groves dotted with beech and black oak. The route here runs over a disused tote road once used by twitch horses to pull out felled timber. Views begin to open up to the west as the trail climbs through a series of switch-backs. Pulling around to the north, you now make the steep scramble up the final rise to the west ledges of Pine Hill.

Once on the ledges, you have superb

views over the Cold River Valley to the hills of the Evans Notch region and some of the major peaks in the Carter-Moriah Range in New Hampshire. In the distance, a few small farms dot the countryside. You may want to rest here a while, enjoying the scene. When you're ready to continue, climb farther eastward on moderate grades along the forested ridge of Pine Hill. The route here runs over several grassy hummocks through birch, oak, balsam, and spruce, then rises again to the more open main summit. Thick mats of moss and reindeer lichen-covered granite form a platform from which you'll enjoy good outlooks to the north. The tiny white flowers of mountain sandwort grow in the clearing. Another 10 minutes of walking along this pleasant ridge brings you to the east summit of Pine, with its fine open ledge and excellent views toward Lord Hill and the mountain country to the northeast and east.

The path next drops quickly downward to the southeast, then turns back north and northeast toward Lord Hill. In the notch area between Pine and Lord Hills, you'll see the unmistakable work of the forester. About 20 years ago, these lands were "regeneration cut" to remove undesirable brush and undergrowth. New forestation has grown densely across the col. The trail drops farther through this zone and crosses pretty Bradley Brook. Look for views back to the ridge from which you just descended. Rise again to the east and cross a gravel road, reentering the woods, and climb Lord Hill northeastward through scattered clearings of low-bush blueberries, sweet fern, and bracken. In a few minutes you'll skirt the true summit of Lord Hill and emerge on the lovely, open ledges of this 1,257-foot mountain.

Below, to the east, you'll spot aptly named Horseshoe Pond, its two prongs running north and south around a peninsula. It's a pretty body of water, and the views to the mountains north and eastward around North Lovell are equally striking. Next, continue up the ledgy rise behind you toward the west and come at once to a junction where a side trail left will take you to the site of an old mineral dig. The largest gem-quality aquamarine and beryl crystals found in North America were uncovered here. This same potassium-feldspar ledge has been a chief source of topaz in Maine.

The Conant Trail heads right and away from the mine link, however, dropping quickly to the north toward Harndon Hill. Entering pine woods, you shortly come to a junction where a trail departs to the right for Horseshoe Pond. Keep left (northwest) at this point, walking through pretty corridors of pine as you head for Harndon Hill on a plateau 1,100 feet in elevation. Stone walls crop up here and there, a reminder that many years ago these hillsides were in pasture, the locations of remote hill farms. You'll cross grown-up old fields, now gone back to the wild in sweet fern, blueberries, and brush.

Roughly ½ mile below the Lord Hill ledges, the Conant Trail pulls to your left and begins its long march westward. The trail slabs along the side of Harndon Hill, but does not ascend to its summit. Work your way westward on a clear trail in mixed-growth forest, staying to the north of the regeneration forest cut to your left. The walking here is fairly level as you hike beside another stone wall under the brow of Harndon Hill. The fragrant smell of young balsam can be picked up on the air. White birches dot a hillside strewn with granite boulders. Another stone wall appears uphill on your right.

Soon you hike past the long-disused Harndon homesite, where the old founda-

The view north from Conant Trail

tion holes and a stone-walled corral are visible. A blueberry field lies beyond the weathered foundation stones. Like its neighbor, Lord Hill, Harndon Hill itself, has been a source of fine gemstones, particularly topaz. You walk on to the west through a corner formed by intersecting stone walls, then bear to the southwest, descending steadily. The trail continues down amid blackberry brambles, then widens in hemlock woods dotted with violets. You're on what was Harndon Hill Road; this remnant of it provides easy walking westward.

A series of springs to your right soon becomes a brook that parallels this grassy road. Passing through a recovering clear-cut, the road widens further and you pass a 200-year-old cemetery. Though badly overgrown, hand-cut headstones and gatestones can be seen. The thought of the families who settled here and made a stand against the mountain is a poignant one; their lives finished, the woods and brush have again taken over.

Continuing downhill, pass a woods road that runs off to your right and soon come to the junction with Hemp Hill Road where you turned earlier. Proceed straight ahead and westward here and you will, in a few minutes, pass the two dwellings you saw earlier. Walking west still, cross the deadwater again and arrive at your parking place.

25

Stone House–White Cairn Loop

Distance (round trip): 4¼ miles

Hiking time: 3 hours

Vertical rise: 1,400 feet

Maps: USGS 7½' Speckled Mountain, Maine; USGS 7½' Wild River, New Hampshire; Chatham Trails Association area map

The Stone House–White Cairn Loop over the south arm of Blueberry Mountain is arguably the prettiest walk in the Evans Notch region. Luckily, it's an easily accessible hike and, in the main, moderate enough in the demands it makes on the hiker to be open to all levels of ability. Nestled at the south end of Evans Notch, this approach to Blueberry Mountain lies between Deer Hill to the south and the higher summits of Ames and Speckled Mountains to the north.

Like most of the walks described in this area, the Stone House–White Cairn Loop is reached from ME 113, the Evans Notch Road, which can be picked up either in Fryeburg to the south or to the north in Gilead at its junction with US 2. Watch for Shell Pond Road on the east side of 113, 1.3 miles north of the AMC Cold River Camp. Head on this dirt road by some mailboxes, pass through a cluster of cabins, and cross a wooden bridge over Bickford Brook. Immediately beyond the brook the road bears to the right and then left, heading east again. You stay with this road for slightly more than 1 mile from the paved surface, and then park to the right just before a locked gate. Be sure to pull off the road so as not to block the gate.

The hike traverses the gravel road past the gate to the east as you walk through some pretty mixed growth and open field. In about ⅓ mile, you'll pass the White Cairn Trail on your left where it enters the road next to a couple of giant hardrock maples. Continue eastward, watching for the beginning of the Stone House Trail on your left just beyond a small white outbuilding.

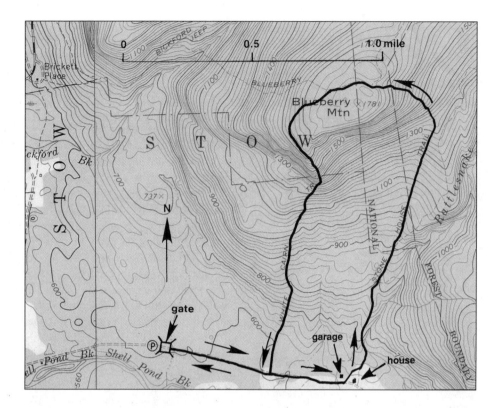

The turn is well marked. Please respect the privacy of the Stone House owners by staying off the grounds as requested.

The route now turns northeast over a winding logging road that sees occasional use. After several turns, the road passes Rattlesnake Brook Flume on your right. Take time to walk over to the stream, as the channel the water has chiseled through the granite is very much worth seeing. A footbridge also crosses the midpoint of the flume. Walking north on the trail again, find a sign pointing to Rattlesnake Pool via a side trail on your right. Take this side trail approximately 150 yards east to the pool and falls, which are even more attractive than the flume below. On a hot day, you may be reluctant to move on.

Resuming your walk, return to the main trail and walk northward on the tote road

through young beech. The route rises gradually but steadily here, and you pass through a grove of balsam just under 1 mile from where you parked. Pulling slightly around to the northwest, walk next through more second-growth hardwood and bear left (west) as the trail leaves the tote road and heads for the summit. The route now becomes quite steep, and the real climbing in this hike takes place in this section.

Norway spruce form an arch over the closely grown trail as you move upward (west). Shortly, the trail climbs onto the open ledges of the summit. The Blueberry Ridge Trail comes in on your right; follow it straight ahead across the broad summit. The highest point on the mountain is marked by a cairn where the Summit Loop Trail begins. This is a good place to rest and enjoy the views to the north over Ames

Looking west from the summit of Blueberry Mountain

and Speckled Mountains (see Hike 26).

The Summit Loop Trail should be passed up in favor of a walk to the west ledges where the Blueberry Ridge Trail starts downhill. You'll have to cover this ground anyway heading for the White Cairn trailhead. Just continue to the west over the summit, dropping briefly into a wooded, boggy depression, and then out onto more granite. A sign indicates the White Cairn Trail on your left. Just ahead there are splendid views to the west and northwest from East and West Royce Mountains down to Mount Meader and the Baldfaces. On a clear fall day with the sun in the west, there are few nicer spots in Evans Notch than right here.

Backtracking a little uphill, bear right (south) on the White Cairn Trail, which marches toward the lower end of the Notch over more red pine–tudded ledges. Walk southwest and south, descending quickly in the open. In ¼ mile you emerge on more attractive ledges with spectacular views over a sheer drop to the southwest, south, and southeast. Deer Hill lies due south, with Harndon Hill and Styles Mountain more around to the southeast and east. Shell Pond is the body of water to the southeast. The trail skirts the edge of the ledges, keeping this panorama in front of you, and then pulls to the east through a stand of white oak.

The trail drops down to the south abruptly, runs through a grove of red pine, and then drops sharply again to the west. More on the level now, you meander to the south, crossing several logging roads that come in from various angles. Be careful not to get sidetracked here. The trail passes through a stand of tall, spindly balsams and then descends to a low, boggy point where it is crossed by another logging road. It is only another 100 yards before you emerge on the gravel road. Bear right for the brief walk back to the gate and your car.

26

Ames and Speckled Mountains

Distance (round trip): 8¼ miles

Hiking time: 5 hours

Vertical rise: 2,150 feet

Maps: USGS 7½' Speckled Mountain, Maine; USGS 7½' Wild River, New Hampshire

At the southern end of Evans Notch stands a fine old brick country house, built in the mid-1800s. It is precisely the kind of place in which one would picture the hardiest of country types braving wild mountain winters. Certainly there was a time when such visions might have accurately reflected life hereabouts. Today, the building serves as headquarters for a Boy Scout council and is manned, in summers, to provide information. But the countryside here in the notch is as wild as ever. It is from the yard of the Brickett Place (as the old house is known) that you'll begin your ascent of Ames and Speckled Mountains.

You've room to park your car near the house just off Evans Notch Road (ME 113), about 11 miles north of Stow. The Bickford Brook Trail leaves the east side of the house yard, and rises quickly southeast and east. At ⅓ mile, your route connects with the Speckled Mountain fire road and turns generally northeast toward the summits. The fire road is a rough grass-and-gravel way, once suitable only for the toughest of four-wheel-drive vehicles, and now closed to all vehicles.

At the ½-mile mark, the trail levels off briefly, and the Blueberry Ridge Trail departs to your right. Continue up the Bickford Brook Trail, and at about ⅔ mile watch for a side path to your right, which will take you out to views of the sand-and-gravel slides that extend down into the Bickford Brook ravine. Just above this side path the fire road crosses several feeder brooks, one or two of which are good sources of water even in dry season.

Another short side trail to your right just

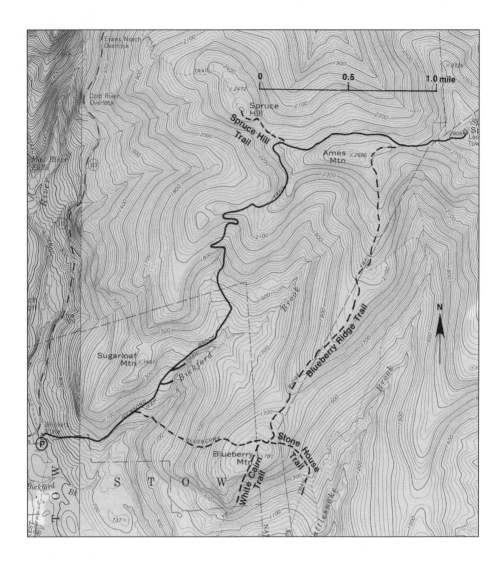

above here leads to good upstream views of Bickford Brook and its falls. You'll get a closer view of the Upper Falls at lookouts just to the right of the trail at about the 1 ¼-mile mark. Listen for the roar.

After leveling off briefly, the trail climbs more steeply northeast, north, and northwest, making two S-curves between the Upper Falls and the 2½-mile point. You climb steadily through the curves, rising up through beech, a belt of evergreens, and then mixed beech and yellow birch. Travel briefly west along the ridge, and, turning northeasterly again, walk down through a depression where the sunlight is filtered by densely grown balsams. The trail narrows in brushy terrain. It is hard to believe that a decade ago this path was wide enough to accommodate trucks and Jeeps.

At 2¾ miles, there are limited views of

Speckled Mountain in late winter

Mount Meader to the west. The Spruce Hill Trail enters from your left as you approach the 3-mile mark. Although you won't notice it, you'll pass the wooded summit of Ames Mountain in the next ¼ mile as the trail slabs eastward toward the summit of Speckled Mountain. You'll get partial views northward into Evans Notch here as the path becomes rougher and rutted.

At 3½ miles, the Blueberry Ridge Trail appears on your right, just as you turn northeastward again for the final rise to the summit of Speckled Mountain. You climb fairly steeply here, past what used to be the last turnaround point for vehicles on the fire road, and move on to the rocky summit crowned by the site of the former fire tower.

The view from Speckled runs from northwest to southeast. The south side of the summit is wooded. What you can see is impressive anyway. East and West Royce Mountains are to the northwest in the foreground, and the Moriahs are just visible behind them and slightly northward. To the north, you can spot the Mahoosuc region; Goose Eye, in particular, stands out. As

Ames and Speckled Mountains

from Caribou Mountain (see Hike 29), Old Speck can be seen if conditions are right.

The horseshoe-shaped formation that is Butters, Red Rock, and Elizabeth Mountains lies to the east. Miles Notch is partly visible if you look to the easternmost end of the low range, where Elizabeth Mountain slopes southward. Looking southeast, you'll note two bodies of water: Virginia and Keewaydin Lakes.

If you return by the same route you climbed, the mountain provides an easy and quick descent. If you want to continue the loop, go down the Blueberry Ridge Trail. You leave the Bickford Brook Trail about ½ mile below the summit at the marker. Your new route turns left and continues southwesterly. The trail rises and falls over a series of slumps for ½ mile, sometimes in the open and sometimes under trees. You pass shortly over open ledges where you should watch carefully for cairns, indicating the route of travel. There are good views in a southerly direction from the ledges. To your left, down in the ravine, is Rattlesnake Brook.

Now on Blueberry Ridge, you descend with slendid views ahead of you. You reach a spring and then climb left to a junction with the Stone House Trail, approximately 2½ miles below the summit. The Blueberry Ridge Trail turns right (westerly) at this point, passes a junction with the White Cairn Trail on your left, and descends westward to Bickford Brook. After descending for nearly a mile, cross Bickford Brook and continue west. Climbing the westerly side of the ravine, join Bickford Brook Trail again 0.9 mile from the Stone House Trail junction, and about ½ mile above the Brickett Place. Arriving shortly on the fire road again, turn left (south) here for the short walk out to Evans Notch Road and the Brickett Place.

27

East Royce Mountain

Distance (round trip): 3 miles

Hiking time: 2½ hours

Vertical rise: 1,700 feet

Maps: USGS 7½' Speckled Mountain, Maine; USGS 7½' Wild River, New Hampshire

With a long enough arm, one could reach out from the summit of East Royce Mountain in Maine and touch New Hampshire air. No legerdemain is involved; it's just that East Royce is probably Maine's western-most elevation. The Maine–New Hampshire border falls between the two peaks of Royce Mountain, with the Maine–or eastern–peak rising imposingly by the center of majestic Evans Notch.

East Royce is not a mammoth mountain, given its immediate 4,000- to 6,000-foot neighbors, but from its 3,100-foot summit, it offers superb views of the Carter-Moriah Range and of the Presidentials beyond. East Royce also provides an excellent outlook to the lower summits to the east in Maine. To the south are North and South Baldface, Eagle Crag, Mount Meader, and the Basin.

The East Royce Trail entrance is well posted on Evans Notch Road (ME 113), about 3 miles north of the Brickett Place (see Hike 26) and Cold River Camp. There is room to leave your car in a grove at the trailhead just off the road on the west side.

The East Royce Trail is barely under way when it crosses the lower reaches of Evans Brook, a stream that begins up on the mountain and flows northerly into the Wild River and the Androscoggin at the head of the notch. After crossing the brook, climb first to your right, and then left (west), ascending the clearly defined track of an old logging road.

In ⅛ mile a water-worn granite ledge marks the second brook crossing. Your path now swings southwest up along the

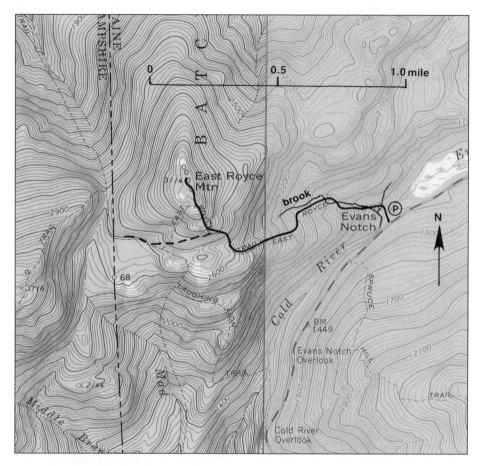

left bank. Continue along the logging road, paralleling the brook and climbing steadily through stands of tall hardwoods and mixed birch. Shortly before you reach the ½-mile point, cross the brook again, turning sharply right (watch for a small arrow on trees). The trail moves northwesterly here over to the main tributary of Evans Brook. In sight of Evans Falls (high on your right), the trail (you are still on the logging road) crosses a feeder brook, swings west again, and ascends an elevated rib of land between the two waterways.

Shortly after passing Evans Falls, the pathway crosses the feeder brook to your left, then continues right (westerly) up

through some fine silver birches as you near the 1-mile mark. Although the old logging road is easily picked out in this section, the brooks are dry in late summer. Brook crossings are less obvious. Watch carefully. The way here is bordered on both sides by handsome clusters of both white and silver birch.

The trail and logging road climb up a steep rise to what must have been a loading area for timber up on the ridge. Birches give way to evergreens here. On the ridge, continue westward and climb through some stone outcrops and low evergreens. The grade here becomes quite steep for about 0.5 mile. The trail levels off briefly

The southeast face of East Royce Mountain

about 1 ¼ miles from the road, where it joins the link to the summit and forms a connector to the Royce and Burnt Mill Brook Trails.

Approximately ¼ mile below the summit, at the junction, a pronounced right turn to the north on a well-defined path begins the ascent of the open ledges that lie below the top. Watch for early southeasterly views framing Spruce Hill and Ames and Speckled Mountains. On the final leg to the top, follow painted blazes and cairns over the ledges to the northwest.

In spring, the summit view to the west reveals the Presidentials in fine alpine garb, white with snow. The summit of Mount Washington is visible over West Royce and Zeta Pass, between South Carter and Mount Hight. South (and left) of Mount Hight is the distinctive shape of Carter Dome. Mount Madison lies west-northwest over North Carter. Adams, Jefferson, and Clay trail off to the west from Madison. Except for some low scrub that screens the view to the north and northeast, you can see in all directions here.

Pass from the south summit to the north crown by following the signs marking the path through the scrub. This short walk is worth the effort, as there are some splendid views to the north and east from the more northerly lookout.

In descending, follow the same route as you did coming up. Keep a cautious eye on the less prominent sections of the trail so you don't miss the turns and crossings.

28

Haystack Notch

Distance (round trip): 10½ miles

Hiking time: 6 hours

Vertical rise: 1,600 feet

Maps: USGS 7½' Speckled Mountain; AMC Carter–Mahoosuc map

The round trip through Haystack Notch amounts to a major woods walk of the kind increasingly hard to find. Though easily walked as a day hike, Haystack Notch lies in wild enough backcountry in the midst of high mountains to give you the feeling of a major expedition. And, if you plan it that way, the journey through Haystack can be extended to a 2-day hike, with an overnight at the Evans Notch end of the trail.

The route through the notch and over a col of Haystack Mountain is a point-to-point hike, running east–west and returning. The walk begins in Mason by the remains of an old farm settlement and runs west along the banks of the West Branch of the Pleasant River, descending gradually beyond Haystack Mountain to Evans Brook in Evans Notch, where it is possible to camp.

This hike makes an excellent walk for the amateur naturalist, too. Rocks, minerals, different bird species, wildlife, and mushrooms and various other fungi are plentiful, and you are very definitely in black bear and moose country while in the Haystack Notch area. You'll find this walk most comfortable in late summer and early autumn. The route crosses many streams, and the walking will be difficult and very roundabout in the wet weather of spring, when many of the brooks are sometimes problematic to cross.

The trailhead for an east–west transit of Haystack is found by leaving US 2 opposite the post office in West Bethel and driving south on Flat Road. Follow this road 6¼ miles, staying on the widest road into Mason. The road becomes gravel as it parallels the West Branch of the Pleasant

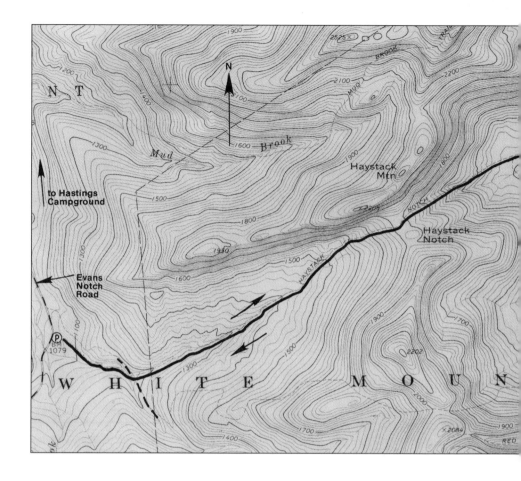

River. Keep right at a well-marked fork in the road and you'll arrive at the forest service trail signs and parking area for both Haystack Notch and the Miles Notch Trail (see Hike 7). If you wish to hike this route in only one direction, you can spot a car at the other end of the trail on ME 113, 6 miles south of its junction with US 2 in Gilead.

From the trailhead, head west through a clearing and along the West Branch of the Pleasant River. In about ¼ mile, pass old cellar holes of a farm settlement and continue west and southwest on a tote road. Shortly, you cross the river several times,

pulling gradually around to the southwest through pretty mixed growth. After walking 1¼ miles westward, you enter White Mountain National Forest lands. Rising very slightly, the route continues to the southwest, staying within the low point of the northern watershed of Butters and Red Rock Mountains to the south.

At 2¼ miles from your car, the trail crosses log culverts and begins to pull away from the West Branch. The grade now runs uphill more noticeably amid maple and beech, the ground dotted with doll's-eye or white baneberry. Several brooks, some

---

Evans Notch Region

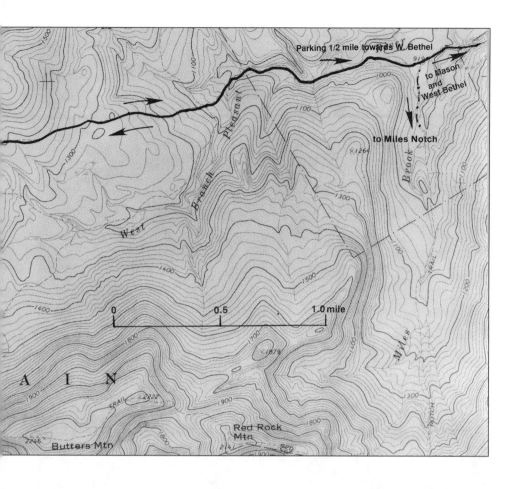

dry, are crossed in this section. Given the variety of hardwoods, this march up toward highest point on this route.

You now descend to the west through aster, starflower, Indian cucumber, and wood sorrel. The trail drops gradually west-southwest over the pegmatitic granite of the mountain and into scattered, very old giant maples, set back among granite boulders. Not quite 4 miles from your starting place, the trail crests a knoll, and a tributary of Evans Brook comes into view. You cross this brook several times, finally bearing right and crossing the brook one final time. Con-tinue west for another ¼ mile and emerge on ME 113 opposite Evans Brook.

A 2½-mile walk north on Evans Notch Road will bring you to the campground in Hastings by the junction of Evans Brook and Wild River. It's a fine place to pitch your tent and rustle up some dinner. Tech-nically, you can camp almost anywhere in the woods along Evans Notch Road (ME 113), as it is all US Forest Service land. There are some restrictions, however, and fire permits may be required in summer. For information and permits, contact the District Ranger, White Mountain National For-

Haystack Notch Trail

est, Gorham, NH 03581 (603-466-2713).

If you decide not to make this an overnighter and don't make the side trip north to Hastings and the campground (which is not included in the mileage estimate for this hike), you'll find plenty of good places to sit and have your lunch along the banks of beautiful Evans Brook before retracing your steps eastward to your car in Mason. Leave early enough on the return, which requires slightly more uphill work, to reach your car before dark.

29

Caribou Mountain

Distance (around loop): 7 miles

Hiking time: 5 hours

Vertical rise: 1,900 feet

Map: USGS 7½' Speckled Mountain

Often, the rewards offered by a mountain are tied to the seasons; some mountains are best climbed at certain times of the year. Caribou Mountain, for instance, deserves your attention in late spring and early summer. Get yourself up into Evans Notch while the last of the snow is still melting, and you're in for something special. Two fine waterways border the trails that form the Caribou loop. Before the warm weather sets in, these streams are running full tilt. They carry the snowmelt down the mountain alongside the trail. And in mid-May, there are few places in Maine I'd rather be.

Morrison Brook and the Caribou Trail interweave nearly to the summit. Along the way, there are some truly scenic cataracts and falls. On the return loop, Mud Brook forms high on the south ridges of Caribou opposite Haystack Mountain and sticks close to Mud Brook Trail all the way out to the Notch Road. Together, the two brooks offer plenty of incentive to hike up Caribou and back, with the fine views from the top providing a special bonus.

The Caribou and Mud Brook Trails leave the east side of Evans Notch Road (ME 113) roughly 6.5 miles north of the Brickett Place and 6.25 miles south of the ME 113–US 2 intersection in Gilead. This new US Forest Service parking area is by the trailhead on the east side of the road. On the ascent, you leave the road and bear left, heading north and northwest parallel to the road. You walk over ½ mile before bearing to the right, crossing Morrison Brook and heading northeast and east toward Caribou Mountain. This is your first glimpse of a

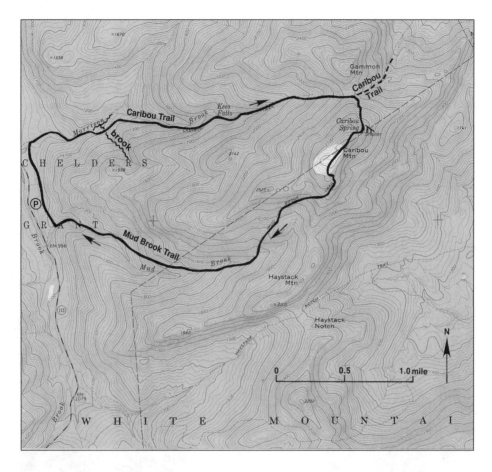

stream that you will rejoin shortly and that you will stay with most of the way to the summit.

Now, proceeding east-southeast, you soon cross the brook again and climb along the east side of the stream. You'll cross several feeder brooks here as they flow in from your right. At slightly over 1 mile, you'll note rows of very tall, old silver and yellow birch. Birches of this size and vintage are uncommon.

Heading due east, you climb steadily now, slabbing along the increasingly steep rise to the right of the trail. Morrison Brook flows at the bottom of the ravine to your left. As you look down from above, the brook

makes a pretty sight—particularly if you've come at the right time of year.

From ¼ to 2 miles along the trail, you walk above a series of cataracts and falls. Kees Falls is seen just past the 1½-mile point, with another cascade (high and to the right of the trail) not far beyond.

Crossing Morrison once more and continuing eastward, you ascend more rapidly now as the trail hugs the left side of the ravine. Good views to the south and southwest emerge, especially if you're climbing in early spring or late autumn. Cross the last feeder brooks that flow into Morrison at about 2½ miles from the road. The trail levels off briefly above here. Climbing again,

---

Morrison Brook along the Caribou Trail

you reach the col between Caribou and Gammon Mountains (there has been some blowdown here in recent years). The Caribou Trail continues straight ahead to Bog Road and West Bethel. Turn right here on the col and ascend Mud Brook Trail to the summit, traveling south and then southwest. A USFS shelter is located nearby between the col and Caribou summit and is a good place to camp if you're planning an overnighter.

Continuing south, climb rapidly through birch and balsam to the first of two open summits beyond the shelter. Proceed past the first clearing, which has views only to the northwest, and you'll arrive shortly at the true summit, which boasts a fine 360-degree view.

Speckled Mountain is the most prominent summit immediately to the south-southwest. Slightly to the left, you see the upper reaches of Kezar Lake and Horseshoe Pond. East Royce Mountain lies across Evans Notch to the southwest. Behind Royce, stretching south to north on the far western horizon, lies the Carter-Moriah Range, topped by Mount Washington, still more distant. Peabody and Pickett Henry Mountains are to the immediate north. If you look between the two on a clear day, you'll see Old Speck far to the north.

To begin your descent via the second half of the Caribou loop, follow the cairns south to an open, lower ledge, where the views to the south and west continue to be excellent, but become more sheltered. The trail meanders over the ledge, briefly turns sharply eastward, and then resumes its course toward the south and southwest through mixed scrub. Watch the cairns carefully as you descend the ledges; it's easy to miss the trail here.

You turn westerly, rapidly descending amid tangled scrub and then through birch

and balsam groves. At slightly less than 1 mile from the summit (2½ miles above the road), the trail crosses two feeder streams that will shortly become Mud Brook—certainly a misnomer, for Mud Brook flows clear and clean from its origins to Evans Brook.

Beyond the streams, the trail proceeds west and northwest, slabbing the side of a ridge opposite Haystack Mountain. There are good views to the south here. The gradual descent continues, as you drop down among tall hardwoods and then walk southwesterly through stands of birch and balsam again. More feeder brooks are crossed (you are now about midway on the trail), after which a steep southerly drop leads you across the brook again. Skirting the west ridge of Caribou, the walkout travels in a northwesterly direction with Mud Brook now on your left.

The final descent is gradual, and you pass through areas cut over for timber years ago. The route follows a logging road that intersects periodically with others, leaving open areas that have become deer pastures. Signs of deer are usually plentiful hereabouts, and you may be fortunate enough to spot a family of whitetails as they come down to the brook at sunset.

You'll keep close to the brook as the trail nears Evans Notch Road. Mud Brook meanders to the south in a wide loop below thick firs and away from the trail momentarily. The trail pulls to the right (north) in a recently relocated section, and makes its way to the parking area where you left your car on the right side of Evans Notch Road.

Recently, Caribou Mountain and surrounding woodlands have been granted a wilderness designation by the federal government. This classification will protect the "backcountry" flavor of these grounds and preserve them, unchanged, for hikers visiting in future years.

30

The Roost

Distance (round trip): 1 mile

Hiking time: 45 minutes

Vertical rise: 400 feet

Map: USGS 7½' Speckled Mountain

There is a kind of justice to mountain climbing: The excellence of the views you get at the top is often proportionate to the amount of effort expended in climbing up. Occasionally there are comfortable exceptions; the Roost is one of them.

The Roost is a small outcrop of ledge, a low summit, at the head of Evans Notch, offering good views south, west, and north. And it's all to be had for an easy climb. Indeed, there are many higher summits in Maine that provide fewer good outlooks.

The Roost Trail begins in the township of Hastings on ME 113 (Evans Notch Road), about 3 miles south of US 2. A spacious camping area lies just south on the Notch Road. The trailhead is located at the junction of the Wild River and Evans Brook, and a more appealing prospect would be hard to imagine. The brook stretches southeasterly toward the Roost and Caribou Mountain, while the Wild River curves upstream and westward toward its origins high in Perkins Notch at Ketchum Pond. Park off the road, south of the bridge.

At ¼ mile, cross a small brook entering from your left. You'll see a giant boulder here to the right of the trail. Climbing through tall white birch, pass a low rock outcrop on your right, and then turn southward into a ledge depression surrounded by balsam and pine growth. This is the first of two ledges that form the Roost. A few yards southwest beyond this point, you'll emerge onto the true Roost, well above Evans Notch Road.

Starting from ME 113 at the north end of

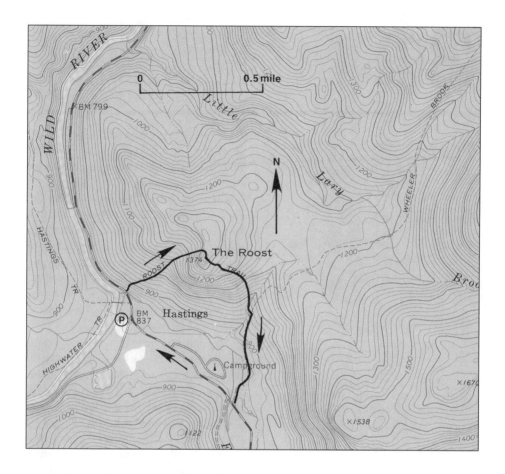

Evans Brook Bridge, ascend the Roost Trail directly up a steep, low ridge. Climbing northeasterly, you reach level ground briefly above the ridge, then turn easterly toward the Roost. Your route is through hardwood groves, with several giant old white pines rising close to the trailside.

This 1,200-foot-high ledge gives you an excellent view through the notch. East and West Royce Mountains rise well to the southwest, across the notch. Howe Peak stands directly opposite your position. Behind Howe Peak, the Moriahs stand out. Look to the far left (southeast) for Caribou Mountain. To the northwest, Baldcap and lower summits lead northeast to Mahoosuc Notch.

From here, there are two routes back to the road and your starting point. You can simply retrace your steps, and arrive back at the trailhead in about 20 minutes. Or you can continue a loop that descends gradually from the south, or far end, of the clearing. This route runs southeast and south, gradually coming around to the southwest and emerging on ME 113 alongside a stream. Turn right on the road, passing the Hastings Campground on your right, and you'll return in minutes to your starting place about ½ mile north.

31

Wheeler Brook

Distance (full circle): 9 miles

Hiking time: 5 hours

Vertical rise: 1,700 feet

Maps: USGS 7½' Gilead; USGS 7½' Speckled Mountain

This route at the north end of Evans Notch offers the hiker a variety of possibilities. With two cars, the trail can be done as an end-to-end walk from US 2 in Gilead to a parking area above Little Lary Brook in what used to be called Batchelders Grant. It is also possible to take the fine walk through the wooded hills that are a source of Wheeler Brook, descending to Evans Notch Road, and then walking that road out to US 2 and back east along US 2 to your starting point. It is this longer (9-mile) circle walk that is described here.

This route provides some climbing on easy grades, a chance to camp if you wish, proximity to several pretty streams, and a fine road walk along the banks of the Wild River. Evans Notch Road is not plowed in winter, and this route also can be used by showshoers and ski tourers who are well equipped and fully experienced in winter tripping. In spring, summer, and fall you may want to do sections of this varied and interesting trail as shorter hikes.

The trail begins on US 2, about 2.2 miles east of the Evans Notch Road intersection in Gilead. Parking is available at the trailhead opposite an old, Colonial-style farmhouse. Watch carefully for signs. Hikers should note that the trailhead area on US 2 may have changed. This spot has been in use intermittently for military training, and some cutting of brush and building of parking areas may result in a minor relocation of the trail's entry point into the woods. Scout the area briefly when you arrive, or call the White Mountain National Forest headquarters in Gorham, New Hampshire

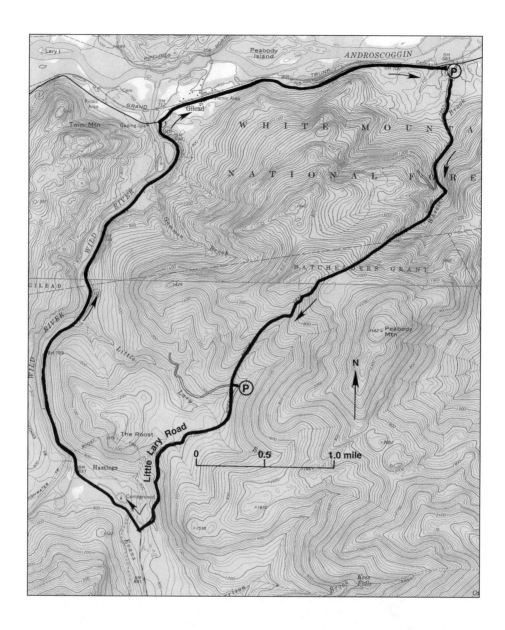

(603-466-2713), for its current status.

The trail begins on a sheltered woods road on the south side of US 2. Heading south, follow the road for about ½ mile. The road makes a sharp turn to the right, but you turn off on a path to the left (southeast). This route crosses Wheeler Brook and pulls southwest, gradually ascending the lower of Peabody Mountain's two summits. This is the highest point in the walk. The actual *second* summit is wooded, so there are no views at this point. (For clear views of this area, see Caribou Mountain and the Roost, Hikes 29 and 30.)

Swift River, Wheeler Brook Loop

Turning to the southwest, you slowly descend the lower reaches of Peabody Mountain, cross Little Lary Brook, which flows into the Wild River, and arrive on Little Lary Brook Road. This gravel road has been well graded and extended nearly to the west slope of Peabody Mountain to support lumbering and gravel mining. The trail outlet at this point varies, as the area has been open to logging and may have been relocated. The trail follows the road from the mountain, through a gate about 1½ miles from Evans Notch Road, and continues to Hastings Campground. The road and trail join Evans Notch Road just south of the campground. At this point, you are about 5½ miles from your car via the tarred road. Campsites are available here at Hastings in summer (check with the caretakers).

To return to Gilead, walk north on Evans Notch Road. Very soon you come to the junction of Evans Brook and the Wild River, opposite the trailhead of the Roost Trail. The river junction makes one of the prettiest sights in the notch. The river views continue as you walk north to Gilead, about 3½ miles from the camping area. This road walk descends continuously as you walk toward Gilead with fine river views most of the way. At Gilead, a highway bridge to your left provides good views along the river, north and south. Turn right and east along US 2 at Gilead, and walk a final 2¼ miles to your car.

As I hinted before, this circle also makes a fine winter outing. A reliable ski-touring pack, with ski slots, is useful for carrying your cross-country skis and gear on the inbound trip over Peabody Mountain. You'll probably want snowshoes on until you reach Little Lary Brook Road. Swap your snowshoes for skis at this point, if you wish, for a good tour. Warm clothing, high-energy foods, an extra ski tip, and spare snowshoe bindings should be taken along for safety if you make the circle in winter. Such a winter trip is for experienced and fit hikers with winter backcountry experience only.

Note: Signs indicating the trailhead on this route seem to change often. A sign showing a hiker has usually been in place at the trailhead in the grassy field opposite the old house noted earlier. The actual trail sign was up in the woods. In recent seasons, a WHEELER BROOK sign has been out near the road. As suggested earlier, scout the location for the current trail entry.

32

Albany Mountain

Distance (round trip): 4 miles

Hiking time: 3 hours

Vertical rise: 1,100 feet

Map: USGS 7½' East Stoneham

Not many people think of Maine lands as being within the White Mountain National Forest (WMNF), but they are. In fact, of the nearly 730,000 acres currently within WMNF boundaries, almost 46,000 are in Maine. Although the highest mountains certainly lie within the New Hampshire acreage, I can promise you, with necessary Maine stubbornness, that the prettiest part of the national forest is in Maine. If you've done some of the preceding climbs in the Evans Notch area, you know what I'm talking about. If not, the quiet beauty of the Crocker Pond–Albany Mountain area will convince you. The Maine section of WMNF seldom gets the crowds that New Hampshire does. This means you'll find it easier to camp on the Maine side of the border. Located on the Albany-Stoneham line, Albany Mountain is a pleasant climb offering good views to the mountains in the Miles Notch area to the west. Camping in an attractive setting is available at Crocker Pond, just beyond the trailhead.

To reach the trail, turn south on Flat Road off US 2 at a store opposite the post office in West Bethel. At about 2.5 miles the main road bears right, while you continue straight ahead on a gravel road. The road shortly intersects another gravel way. *Continue straight on.* Approximately 4 miles from West Bethel, a well-marked entrance road to Crocker Pond leads to your right. Turn here, and in another 0.5 mile you'll arrive at the trailhead, which is prominently marked by US Forest Service signs. The Crocker Pond camping area is about 0.75 mile farther along this road. Park well

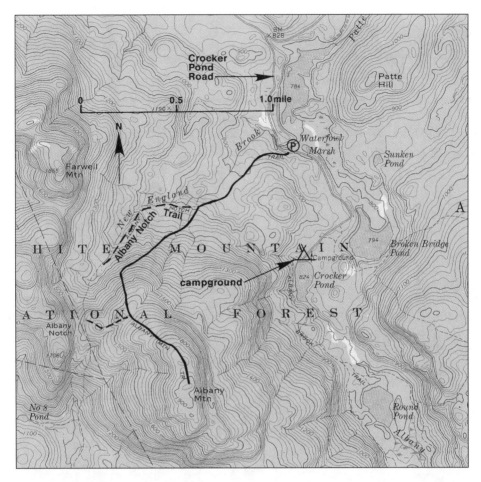

off the road here on the grassy shoulder to the west or leave your car at Crocker Pond.

From the Crocker Pond Road, take the Albany Notch Trail west and southwest along a grass-grown logging road. The grade is slight to the ½-mile point, where the Albany Notch Trail continues straight ahead over a brook, and the Albany Mountain Trail begins turning left. You make the turn left (south), and ascend the north ridge of the mountain gradually, walking up through mixed evergreens and hardwoods. The area is thick with white pine. The Albany Mountain Trail continues southwest and then southeast as it approaches the summit.

About ½ mile north of the summit, a marked trail runs west to Albany Notch. The Albany Mountain Trail proceeds across periodic open ledges and through clumps of blueberry bushes. Watch for any unmarked paths to the right here that lead to an outlook on the ledges to the west. You reach the summit about 2 miles from the road. The best views are from the ledges just crossed, with the hills to the west that form Albany and Miles Notches the most notable. Elizabeth, Red Rock, and Butters Mountains run west beyond Miles Notch,

Crocker Pond

which is due west. Durgin and Speckled Mountains are the two higher summits to the west-southwest. Songo Pond in Albany is the body of water about 5 miles to the northeast.

Now, about those blueberries. If you've had the foresight to bring a pail up the mountain, the reward is at hand. A bushwhack around the summit will usually turn up enough berries for a good Maine blueberry pie or two. My problem has always been the picking. I hate it. Don't have the patience. But if you do, and the season is right—usually mid- to late July—you just may go away with a bucketful.

Retrace your steps for a leisurely walk to your car, about 1 hour.

VI

The Mahoosucs

33

Mount Carlo–Goose Eye Loop

Distance (around loop): 7¼ miles

Hiking time: 6 hours

Vertical rise: 2,200 feet

Maps: USGS 7½' Gilead, Maine; USGS 15' Old Speck Mountain, Maine; USGS 7½' Shelburne, New Hampshire; USGS 15' Milan, New Hampshire

The land that lies north and east of the Androscoggin River along the Maine–New Hampshire state line is both wild and mountainous. The Maine side of this region remains the more isolated of the two. Thus, most of the good Maine climbing in this area is accessible only from lumber company roads leading in from New Hampshire. The Mahoosuc Range in Maine, from Mount Carlo north to Old Speck, lies mainly in lands owned by the former James River Company paper empire. These borderlands are open to the public and, at present, permits or fees are not required.

Mount Carlo provides an excellent day's climb with fine views northeast toward Rangeley in Maine and also south toward the Moriahs and Presidentials in New Hampshire. This hike takes you up and beyond Carlo, along the Mahoosuc Trail (Appalachian Trail), to Goose Eye Mountain. It then heads southwest out to the road on the Goose Eye Trail. The loop makes for a trip of over 7 miles and some of the best views in the Mahoosucs.

Your route into the mountains begins in New Hampshire. From downtown Berlin, cross the Androscoggin River at the lights on Main Street at the north end of the shopping district. After crossing the river, turn right onto Hutchins Street, which soon loops leftward around to the north, crosses a railroad spur, and enters the James River Company pulp yards. Watch for a gravel road that goes off to your right (northeast) within this pulp yard. Turn here and follow unmarked Success Pond Road. This 14-mile gravel road offers access to climbs

Goose Eye Mountain, Mahoosuc Range

throughout the Mahoosuc region. Indeed, except for the long, recently trailed walk-in from Ketchum via Goose Eye Brook and Bull Branch, Success Pond Road furnishes the only way into these mountains. (For directions to Success Pond Road from its northern end in Grafton Notch see Hike 34.)

Watch for the Carlo Col Trail on your right, about 8.5 miles from the beginning of Success Pond Road. There's limited room to pull a car off the road on either shoulder near the trail sign. Make sure you don't block the main right-of-way, as this road is used by big logging trucks.

Both the Carlo Col Trail and the Goose Eye Trail run together southeastward off Success Pond Road for a short distance. Arriving momentarily at a T, the Carlo Col Trail turns sharply right and, on a bridge, soon crosses a brook. Once on the other side, the trail pulls left (eastward), following the route of an old logging road.

At ⅔ mile, you walk more toward the south as the trail pulls away from the south branch of Stearns Brook, which it has followed to this point. A feeder brook joins the trail a short distance above this turn. At ¾ mile, you enter a clearing where logging roads intersect. The col between Mount Carlo and Mount Success is visible high up ahead. Staying to the left, cross the brook here and climb easily through young cherry growth. Among the young trees in this field returning to woods, I've seen many clear moose tracks. Though the field is removed from the swamp browse that moose love, this seems to be a well-used area. Keep your eyes open.

You now begin to climb more steeply, slabbing up a ridge and moving past the junction (left) of another logging road. From

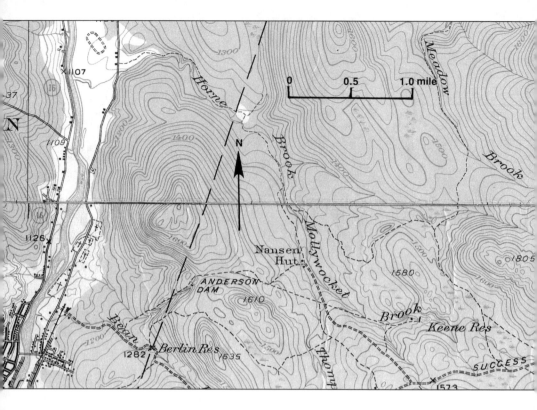

here, your route makes a beeline straight for the col. The logging road diminishes to only a wide path at 1¾ miles, where you cross a small brook. There are several old pines that have grown atop boulders in this section of the trail.

You cross another small brook at the 2-mile mark, and the steeper ascent of the col itself begins. The trail winds up through stands of white birch and fir here. Cross a third brook as you swing more toward the summit of Carlo. Good views of the northwest ridge of Mount Success emerge behind you at this point.

The Carlo Col Shelter stands on your left up on a bluff as you reach a spot ¼ mile below the highest point of the col. Continu-

ing, you soon reach the Mahoosuc Trail in a sharp rock cut at 2⅔ miles. The route to Carlo and Goose Eye turns left. Following this route, ascend northeasterly on a steep grade for ½ mile through close-grown red and black spruce to the Carlo summit.

Low scrub grows around the summit of Carlo. You'll need to move around for outlooks in all directions. To the north is the horn of Goose Eye Mountain. The Mahoosuc Trail proceeds northeast across the sedge.

You may want to make an overnighter of this trip, descending again to Carlo Col Shelter for the night. Sleeping space in the shelter is limited, but there are places for tents, too. Whether you camp overnight or

The Mahoosucs

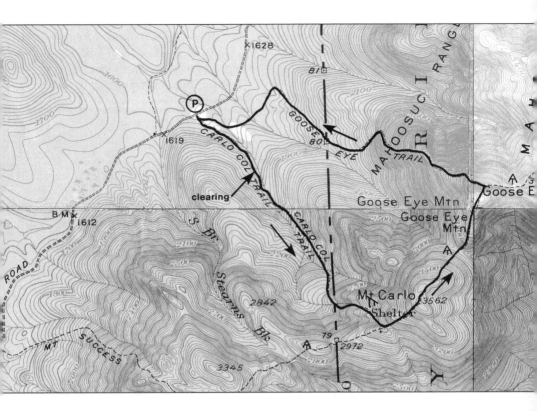

proceed to Goose Eye the same day, head northeast on the Mahoosuc Trail once under way. The trail winds beyond Carlo's summit and enters low evergreens again. You soon pass over the wooded north summit of Carlo and then descend sharply to a col. The trail traverses a series of ledgy areas and low cliffs as it climbs rapidly up the south ridge of Goose Eye. The going here is quite steep, sometimes requiring handholds. Reaching the bare south shoulder of the Eye, turn left on the Goose Eye Trail to the west summit of the mountain, which you'll reach in a few yards. Total distance from the top of Carlo to the west peak of Goose Eye adds up to about 1½ miles. Excellent views in all directions prevail here.

To regain the road, continue the loop by heading down northwestward along the Goose Eye Trail. Use caution on the descent of this steep, ledgy ridge just below the summit. Continuing toward the northwest, you enter the woods. The trail soon bears more to the west as it drops down toward the road on a comfortable grade. Slightly over 1 mile below the summit, the trail makes a sharp turn to the left through country well populated with moose. The spruce and balsam that characterize the upper slopes now give way to hardwoods.

Gradually turning more toward the northwest again, you join the roadbed of an old logging railway about 1 mile above the road. Here, turn again sharply toward the southwest and, following the old railroad bed, reach Success Pond Road and your car.

Note: If it is storming with high winds, don't attempt to climb the exposed area around the summit of Goose Eye. Rather, head down below the timberline, retracing your route on the Carlo Col Trail. Hikers should also be aware that logging occurs in this section from time to time and trail relocations may occur.

34

Mahoosuc Notch and Speck Pond Loop

Distance (around loop): 11 miles

Hiking time: 9 hours

Vertical rise: 2,300 feet

Maps: USGS 15' Old Speck Mountain, Maine; USGS 7½' Gilead, Maine; USGS 15' Milan, New Hampshire; USGS 7½' Shelburne, New Hampshire

The climb in to Speck Pond via Mahoosuc Notch makes a long, very rugged day hike or a leisurely paced but still challenging overnighter through some of Maine's most interesting mountain terrain. This route follows the Appalachian Trail (AT) through the granite rubble of Mahoosuc Notch, the section of the trail that many hikers consider the most difficult. Speck Pond, your destination, is a serene, small body of water located in a 3,500-foot-high basin, between Mahoosuc Arm and Old Speck Mountain. The traverse of the notch provides some of the most unusual, if demanding, hiking in eastern America. Fine views of the pond and its northerly neighbor, Old Speck, are seen on both the approach and the return as you go over Mahoosuc Arm.

This long circuit in the northern end of the Mahoosucs is most easily approached from ME 26 in Grafton Notch. Take ME 26 north from its junction with ME 5 in Newry, or south from its junction with NH 16 in Errol, New Hampshire. Watch for Success Pond Road on the west side of ME 26, approximately 2.5 miles north of the Appalachian Trail crossing in Grafton Notch, and roughly 5 miles south of Upton center. (For an approach to this trailhead from the west via Berlin, New Hampshire, and Success Pond see Hike 33.)

Head west and southwest on this gravel road as it runs past York Pond and crosses Black Brook. The road pulls southward and passes the Speck Pond Trail on your left, 7.5 miles from ME 26. (You'll emerge here on the return part of this demanding loop hike and walk the road south back to your

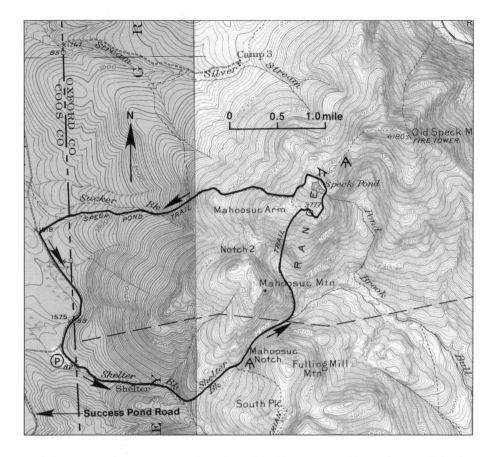

car.) You soon pass a spur to your right that ends at Success Pond; continue further southward 1.5 miles. Here, locate the short turn-in to the Notch Trail on your left—the east side of Success Pond Road. Drive in just 0.1 mile and park in a grassy lot. (Some relocation has occured here in recent years. Watch for signs.)

The Notch Trail crosses a shallow brook and follows a little-used tote road to the south-southeast. You shortly cross a second brook and reach a broad clearing with an old house. Passing a grove of aspens, leave the road and make an abrupt *left* just beyond the clearing. Here the trail runs east-southeast and east up slight grades on an unused fire road bordered with great clusters of

blackberry bushes. The path soon rejoins the brook on your left, which it recrosses in about ½ mile, continuing eastward.

You'll cross the brook twice again as you walk eastward, finally following a small inlet to the left (north) of a series of open barrens. The trail levels off on this height-of-land, meandering northeastward through a deciduous forest to a junction with the Appalachian Trail 2½ miles from your starting point. *Note:* The Appalachian Trail (AT) is known as the Mahoosuc Trail in this section and is referred to by that name on trail markers along the path.

From the trail junction, head left (north) on the Mahoosuc Trail (AT). You drop down immediately into the trench of the notch.

Speck Pond

The air temperature changes suddenly, often being 10 or 20 degrees cooler than on the trail you just left, however warm the day. Snow lingers here until well into summer. The route proceeds over huge slabs of rock that have fallen from the sides of Mahoosuc and Fulling Mill Mountains and is marked by a series of white blazes. For more than 1 mile, you clamber to the northeast over and under this great jumble of rock. *Use extra caution in this section; rock surfaces may be slippery, and the danger of losing your footing and dropping into a hole is constant.* A small, soft pack

works well in the notch, as larger frame packs are very difficult to maneuver through the boulder caves, and in some places may prove a real hindrance.

In the notch, the route gradually descends, joining a brook near the lower end. Emerging from the cleft between the mountains, move away from the brook and left (northwest), climbing the east side of Mahoosuc Mountain and then northward up Mahoosuc Arm. As you move onto the arm, you briefly follow an old logging road; the trail then crosses a brook into a lumbered area. From here, you climb on increasingly stiff grades through balsam and red spruce, ascending sharply over the boulders and ledges that characterize the top of the arm.

The views south from the bare summit of Mahoosuc Arm are excellent. Here, from your platform of folded, metamorphosed rock, you can see back down into the notch. Rock slides on Fulling Mill Mountain and open ledges on Mahoosuc Mountain mark the portals of the notch. To the north lies the rolling expanse of Old Speck. Slide Mountain and Riley Mountain are the two summits nearby to the east, and behind them rests the long, rangy summit of Sunday River Whitecap.

Head right (north) on the Mahoosuc Trail toward Old Speck. You'll drop rapidly down to Speck Pond, approaching the water from its south end. Follow the northeast shore of the pond around to Speck Pond Shelter. The shelter and several tent platforms provide overnight accommodations. Located right on the shore, this site makes a very attractive camp. Because of heavy use, particularly by "through hikers," the shelter is usually supervised by a caretaker during the peak months of June, July, and August. A small fee is charged for overnight stays. (Pack in your own gear and food.) The shelter area provides a pleasant spot to have your lunch if you're planning to hike out again the same day. (For over-nighters, this is a good base camp from which to climb Old Speck via the west ridge above the pond. For information on the status of camping at Speck Pond call the US Forest Service in Gorham, New Hampshire or the Appalachian Mountain Club, also in Gorham.)

To return to Success Pond Road, take the Speck Pond Trail as it departs northwest from the shelter. You turn shortly, climbing very steeply southwest to the summit of the arm. Look back for frequent superb views of the pond and Old Speck, which are particularly striking at late afternoon in good weather. In about 1/3 mile, pass the May Cutoff on your left. Stay *right* here, proceeding downward on the Speck Pond Trail to the west and southwest.

The descent runs first through tall groves of beautiful balsam, leveling off briefly on the north end of a ridge (2,950 feet). Slabbing downward to the southwest, you descend through evergreens and mixed hardwoods, where open patches permit good views to the area west of Success Pond. The descent becomes gradually less steep, entering an area where you cross several logging roads. Keep a sharp lookout for trail blazes here, as it's easy to wander off the path. One mile above the road, the path joins the route of a prominent logging road, moving to the northwest and then around to the southwest. Bluets and painted trillium border the path, and moose footprints and droppings are frequently spotted.

In minutes, you join another logging right-of-way and emerge on a gravel road. Turn left here and follow this road south a short distance to where it intersects Success Pond Road. Continue south on Success Pond Road to the Notch Trail sign where you left your car (about 1 1/2 miles).

35

Old Speck

Distance (round trip): 7½ miles

Hiking time: 6 hours

Vertical rise: 2,730 feet

Maps: USGS 15' Old Speck Mountain, Maine; USGS 15' Milan, New Hampshire

Maine's third highest mountain (after Katahdin and Sugarloaf) will give you something to sink your teeth into. Whether you're determined to head straight up or to make the long traverse of the north ridge, Old Speck provides the kind of hiking experience that lets you know you're in Maine. The mountain rises high over Grafton Notch and is reached via ME 26 from Bethel. Overnight camping is available on a first-come, first-served basis at Grafton Notch Shelter on the Appalachian Trail, about 2½ miles east of the Old Speck trailhead.

The trail system on the mountain and in the notch has undergone some changes, and you should be aware that old maps may not have an accurate picture of available routes up the mountain. The Old Speck Trail, once known as the Fire Warden's Trail, now runs slightly north of the old route, and begins at a parking area on ME 26 a bit less than 3 miles north of Screw Auger Falls and about 12 miles northwest of Bethel. The old, badly eroded fire warden's route is no longer in use. The "new" Old Speck Trail includes parts of the former Cascade Brook Trail, the Eyebrow Trail, the Upper Ridge Link Trail, and the Skyline Trail. The route is clearly marked and there is a map of the route on a trail board at the parking area. The Old Speck Trail is the current route of the Appalachian Trail.

From the north side of the parking area, the Old Speck Trail runs west nearly on the level, bears left at a fork where the Eyebrow Trail comes in from the right, and climbs

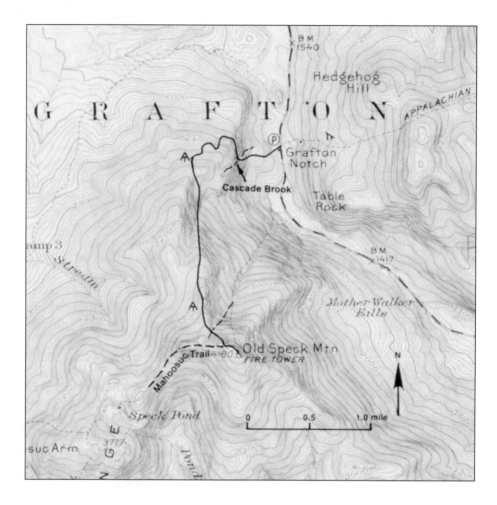

easily in the direction of the summit. Heading south-southwest, you cross Cascade Brook. Several feeder brooks are soon passed. Turn around to the north, slabbing the ridge as the trail runs through the first of two north–south S-curves. Passing close to the lower cascades on your right, proceed southwest again, then turn north through the second S and head west, rising quickly to the left of the cascades.

The upper reaches of the brook are followed to approximately the ¾-mile point, where the trail turns sharply right, crosses the brook, and moves northward along ledges toward the Eyebrow. There are excellent views down the valley in this section.

To continue toward the summit, follow the Old Speck Trail through an evergreen grove north and northwest, then swing west up the ridge to the uneven timberline. At 1½ miles, open spaces provide views of the summit approximately 2¼ miles away. A long ridgewalk takes you through forests of red spruce, over a series of hummocks and bare ledges.

At ¾ mile below the summit, pass the Link Trail down to the site of the old fire warden's cabin. The Old Speck Trail dips

Storm clouds atop Old Speck

into a final depression before rising sharply to a junction with the Mahoosuc Trail, which runs right to Speck Pond Shelter (see Hike 34). Turn left here and, passing the disused old Fire Warden's Trail on your left, arrive in about ¼ mile at the 4,180-foot summit.

A rebuilt observation tower on the summit is worth a careful climb, for the views run 360 degrees and are outstanding. You can look to the southwest directly down Mahoosuc Notch, framed by Mahoosuc and Fulling Mill Mountains. The twin peaks of Baldpate rise strikingly to the northeast; Dresser and Long Mountains are due east; Slide Mountain and Sunday River Whitecap are to the southeast. On a clear day, if you look beyond Baldpate, the mountains of the Rangeley region—particularly Saddleback—stand out. There is plenty of room on the wooded summit to stretch out or prepare lunch, and you may encounter a large, friendly rabbit with whom I've had several one-sided conversations.

Make the return trip by retracing your steps to ME 26. Although technically possible, returning to the road via the old Fire Warden's Trail is definitely not recommended.

36

Baldpate Mountain

Distance (round trip including Table Rock): 8½ miles

Hiking time: 6½ hours

Vertical rise: 2,700 feet

Map: USGS 15' Old Speck Mountain

Grafton Notch remains a place to gladden the heart of civilization haters. It's a remote region, unspoiled and just enough out of the way to have escaped the tourist hordes and developers. Grafton Notch Road (ME 26) meanders through some beautiful farm country and between the mountains. There are some streams along here, too, that harbor their share of trout, and moose are seen often. In short, the notch provides some robust hiking in a very attractive western Maine setting.

The Appalachian Trail (AT), the route for this hike, ascends Baldpate from ME 26 in Grafton Notch opposite the parking area for Old Speck (Hike 35). In recent years the route has been relocated, and shelter access changed to eliminate wear on older sections of the trail. The new section of the AT begins on the east side of the road and runs east-northeast across a grassy marsh area and into a grove of spruce and hardwoods. The newly constructed loop to Table Rock is passed on the right in a few minutes. Keep on the main trail and save the side trip to Table Rock for the return.

Continuing upward on the white-blazed AT, you shortly reach one of the feeder brooks that spill into the Bear River. The route now broadens, meandering southeast and northeast through mixed growth, reaching the Table Rock Trail at just under 1 mile. The Table Rock Trail leads to the right almost due south, and takes you to some of the finest views in the notch. This side trail rises easily southward through slender hardwoods, crosses a rivulet, and then climbs somewhat more

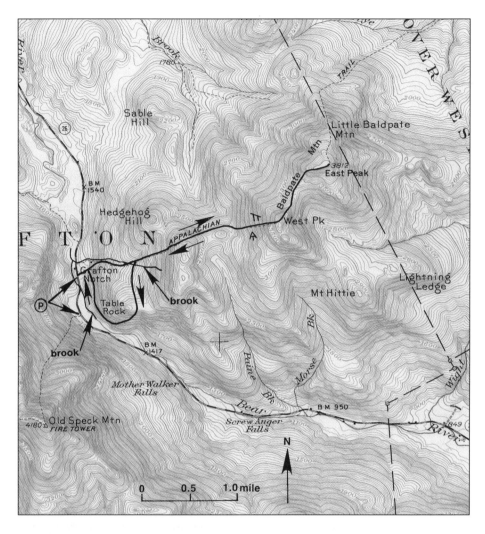

Map labels: OVERWES · River · Brook · 1780 · 1900 · 2000 · Sable Hill · 26 · Little Baldpate Mtn · B M 1540 · TRAIL · Baldpate Mtn · 3812 East Peak · Hedgehog Hill · APPALACHIAN · TT A · West Pk · Lightning Ledge · FTON · Crafton Notch · brook · Table Rock · Mt Hittie · P · brook · B M 1417 · Paine Bk · Morse Bk · Widl · Mother Walker Falls · Bear · Old Speck Mtn 4180 FIRE TOWER · Screw Auger Falls · B M 950 · River · 1849 · N · 0   0.5   1.0 mile · 1500

steeply up a dome to the table. This short detour is worth the walk, for views of old Speck, Sunday River Whitecap, and Puzzle Mountain (way down the Bear River Valley) are truly excellent. The distance from the AT to the table and back is under 1 mile.

Back at the trail junction, continue rightward up Baldpate and, crossing a brook, follow the trail as it rises to the east through bushes that nearly obscure the path in midsummer. The going here may be wet. This is also prime country for moose-spotting.

The enormous animals, more shy now that they are being hunted in Maine again after a 30-year hiatus, like the succulent young browse that characterizes this section of the trail. The old shelter, formerly located near ME 26, has been removed. A new one is now located below Baldpate's west summit.

At about 2½ miles above the road, the trail runs more to the east and southeast as it climbs a low knob. Just before you begin the brisk ascent of this ledgy knob, you will pass the new shelter. Though roomy, it is

The west and east peaks of Baldpate

likely to be heavily used in summer, and packing along a lightweight tent may be in order if you are hiking on weekends. The summit of the west peak is reached at 3 miles from the trailhead. Views to the northwest open up as you cross the west summit and continue northeastward along a ridge. You drop down to a depression, cross a brook, and begin the steady ascent of Baldpate's east peak. There are open spots here with good views. Moving eastward still, you climb over open ledges and reach the east peak at a bit more than 3¼ miles.

The outlook makes the long trudge in from the road seem trifling. You can look northward over Little Baldpate and Surplus Mountains, which create a watershed for eastward-running Frye Brook. The bare summit of Sunday River Whitecap, due south over Mount Hittie, is visible, as are Dresser and Long Mountains in an arc to the southeast. Black Mountain and Gregg Mountain are the two low summits immediately to the east-northeast. Old Speck looms to the southwest.

The trip back to the road is made by retracing your steps. If you did not make the side trip to Table Rock on the ascent, it can be made on your way down. Turn left on the Table Rock side trail. For an added challenge, after visiting the table, follow the blue-blazed loop trail, which ascends the steep terrain beneath the table and rejoins the AT just east of the road roughly opposite from where you parked.

VII

Mount Desert Island–Acadia National Park

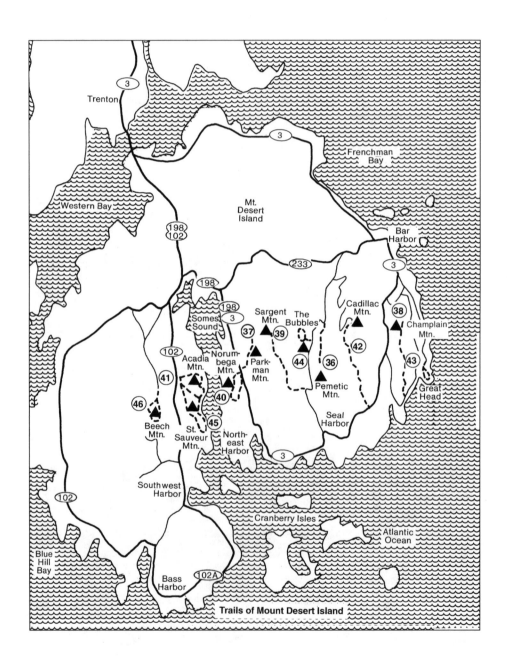

Trails of Mount Desert Island

Introduction

Mount Desert is the largest coastal island in Maine. Its kidney-shaped land mass lies off Trenton at the head of Frenchman Bay, east of Blue Hill and west of Schoodic Point. A heavily glaciated, mountainous island, Mount Desert makes a spectacular destination for the hiker. Clearly marked, highly attractive trails ascend to dozens of well-placed summits scattered all over the island. Shore rambles and strolls through small villages provide pleasant walking, too. The natural beauty of Mount Desert defies easy description; to say that it has few equals anywhere in America isn't hyperbole. The trail descriptions in this section provide a thorough introduction to the best of Mount Desert Island, but you'll have to see for yourself.

The lands of Acadia National Park are at the core of Mount Desert's natural attractiveness. The park is a sort of enclave within the larger boundaries of the island and contains all of the walks in this section. Some of the trails are reached only by the park service road, which may be entered at Hulls Cove in the north or at other points on the island. An entrance fee must be paid to use this road and other park facilities. Other hikes on the island are reached on toll-free state roads (see each hike description for access directions). Acadia also features campgrounds, picnic areas, boat-launch ramps, and beaches. A complete guide to park facilities may be found at the Hulls Cove entrance. Russell Butcher's *Guide to Acadia National Park,* available in local stores, is must reading.

The best time to visit Mount Desert is during the months of October through May. High summer tends to be crowded, and the island's narrow roads fill up with that quintessential American phenomenon, the motorized sightseer. You won't see this person on the trails, for he never gets far from an automobile. He does, however, make it harder to get to that trailhead you're in search of. If you visit Acadia in the off-season, you'll find nary a person in the woods and that serene beauty for which Acadia is famous won't be overrun with motorbound visitors. There are plenty of accommodations in the Ellsworth–Mount Desert region. Indeed, they are too plentiful and draw more congestion each year. Park service officials are urging local merchants not to overbuild, but, rather, to accommodate more people in the off-seasons. I concur with this advice, and you can do your part in preventing overuse by visiting from after Labor Day up until Memorial Day.

Mount Desert and Acadia offer some fine terrain for the winter snowshoer or cross-country skier. The carriage roads are ideal for ski touring, and portions of most of the walks in this section can be snowshoed in-season. The summits are often icy and blown free of snow in winter, so good boots and instep crampons (available at most mountaineering stores) are advisable. Don't let winter drive you away, though; it's a spectacularly pretty time of year on the island.

Bicyclists will enjoy Acadia, too, as many of the carriage roads make excellent bike routes, and the loop around Eagle Lake has been specially graded for cycling.

The shore at Northeast Harbor

The 43 miles of carriage roads are not open to motorized vehicles, so the cyclist can enjoy the tranquillity he or she craves.

For further information, write to the Superintendent, Acadia National Park, Bar Harbor, ME 04609. If you plan to camp in Acadia, write in advance for reservations.

Note: Several hikes require an approach via the park service road. This is a toll road with fees charged to support year-round maintenance. A week-long pass is available that makes it possible to visit on multiple days (and multiple hikes) at reasonable cost.

37

Pemetic Mountain

Distance (round trip): 2¼ miles

Hiking time: 2 hours

Vertical rise: 950 feet

Maps: USGS 15' Acadia National Park and Vicinity; AMC map of Mount Desert Island

Rising nearly in the center of Mount Desert's "eastern half," Pemetic Mountain provides some excellent views east toward Cadillac and west to Sargent Mountains, and to the parklands to the north on Eagle Lake. A bit out of the way and less frequented than some other climbs on the island, Pemetic offers you exceptional rewards as a first, short hike.

The Pemetic Mountain Trail, which runs the full length of the ridge and terminates at ME 3 in Seal Harbor, begins at the north end of Bubble Pond. To reach Bubble Pond, go south on the park service road, which leaves ME 3 at park headquarters above Hulls Cove (northwest of Bar Harbor). Park your car in the area provided at the north shore of the pond (off the park service road). *Note:* The park service road is a toll road.

The name Pemetic derives from local Native American parlance, meaning simply "a range of hills." From the north end of the pond, you head southwesterly, traveling along the west shore briefly, passing through cedar groves, then turning due west and crossing over one of the many carriage roads that traverse the island.

Past the road, you swing southwest again, walking easily through a second cedar grove at ⅓ mile. Passing through a range of some fine, tall firs, you begin to climb more steadily, moving south-southwesterly toward the summit. This area is densely grown with evergreens and provides some truly pleasant walking. It's a movie-set kind of forest. At ⅔ mile, the trail runs more southerly, passing a boulder-

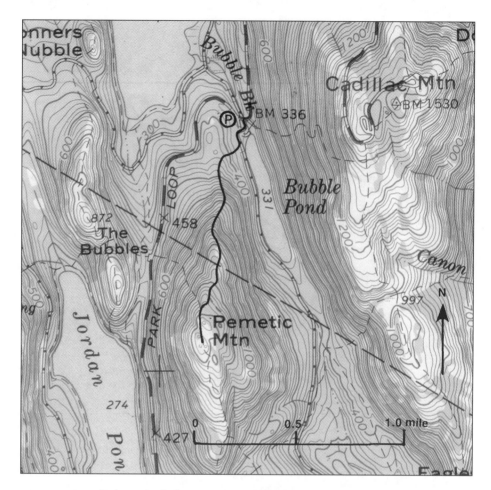

strewn way and along the ledges on the east side of the mountain. There is a good view of Cadillac Mountain to your left as you walk this section.

Turning more westerly, the trail soon brings you to a second ledgy area, where outlooks to the north appear. On clear days, when weather isn't "making" in the valleys, good views of Eagle Lake are yours here. Continuing in the same direction, the second, more open, summit will be reached in about 1/8 mile.

From the summit, the striking, bare ridge to the west is Penobscot and Sargent Mountains. Almost due north of the

Pemetic summit, you can see the full length of Eagle Lake, while to the east and northeast is the long rise of Cadillac Mountain. The open ledges on which you're standing are extensive and make for interesting exploring. There are several good spots on the ledges to rest and have lunch before heading down.

In descending to Bubble Pond on your return, watch the trail carefully. The dense growth makes it easy to take a wrong turn as you head down. Cairns and red blazes help mark the trail. A general northeast course cannot fail to bring you to the road should you lose the trail.

170

Looking north through morning mist toward Eagle Lake

38

Parkman Mountain and Bald Peak

Distance (round trip): 2½ miles

Hiking time: 2 hours

Vertical rise: 700 feet

Maps: USGS 15' Acadia National Park and Vicinity; AMC map of Mount Desert Island

On a sunny, summer day at the height of the season, when many of Mount Desert's trails may have more hikers on them than you care to contend with, two low summits northeast of the Hadlock ponds make an excellent hike. Parkman Mountain and Bald Peak form the west leg of a triangle with Penobscot and Sargent Mountains and furnish fine vantage points over lands to the north and west of the island. These two mountains are really no more than hills, but the easy hike into both provides pleasant walking over varied terrain, and you're likely to have the summits pretty much to yourself.

To reach the trailhead, drive west from Bar Harbor on ME 233 or east from Somesville on ME 198. At the junction of the two roads, continue south on ME 198 for about 3 miles, watching for the parking lot by the trailhead on the east side of the road. You may also reach this spot by driving north on ME 198 from Northeast Harbor.

A rough trail runs almost directly up Parkman, but it is hard to find and poorly marked. A more reliable route begins at the northeast corner of the parking area on a short link to a carriage road. Take this link and turn right, walking uphill to the southeast, arriving in minutes at a junction. Bear sharply *left* at the junction, continuing upward on another unpaved road through a long S-curve. At the top of the curve, about ¼ mile above, watch for trail signs on your left.

Turn off the road at the trail signs and walk northwest over a ledgy shelf through groves of jack pines. The trail recrosses the road at the top of the rise and, turning more northward, enters the woods again. Your

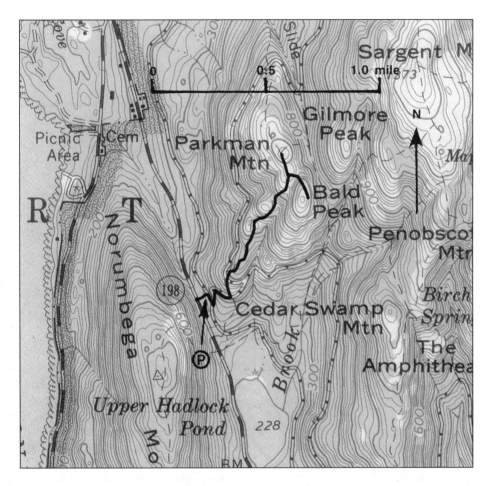

route here lies over more sandy ledge amid thin, mixed growth and curves gradually around to the east. The trail shortly passes through a grove of cedars, and levels off briefly, running east-northeast. Early views of Bald Peak's summit may be had here. The trail is marked with small cairns and paint blazes.

Approximately ⅔ mile from the parking area, a more pronounced scramble up the rocks begins, with occasional views to the north opening up. You drop briefly into a depression and then climb briskly eastward on a series of bare ledges. Excellent views of both Upper and Lower Hadlock Ponds

emerge in this section. In minutes, you slab east-northeast over a knob and above a shallow ravine to your right. The ridge, with Parkman Mountain to your left and Bald Peak to your right, lies just above with fine outlooks to the northwest and west as you ascend.

At the top of the ridge, a link trail runs south-southeast to Bald Peak. Turn right here, dropping into a wooded cleft between the two summits. The link rises quickly, and in ¼ mile you crest the granite summit of aptly named Bald Peak. Excellent views of the Hadlock ponds and the lowlands down the valley to Northeast

Parkman and Bald Mountains over Upper Hadlock Pond

Harbor are to the south here. Greening Island and the open Atlantic lie to the south-southwest. Immediately to the west over the arm of land you have just climbed, you will see the north-south expanse of Norumbega Mountain (see Hike 41). Penobscot and Cedar Swamp Mountains are to the east and southeast.

To reach Parkman Mountain, retrace your steps to the ridgetop trail junction, then turn right (northward) on the trail over the ledges. You'll arrive on Parkman's 940-foot summit in moments. From this totally bare mound of rock, you have a superb vantage point over the northern reaches of Somes Sound and, beyond Somesville, Western Bay. On clear days, you can also see Blue Hill, Bald Mountain, and Mount Waldo on the mainland to the west. The low summit of Acadia Mountain is visible over the northern flanks of Norumbega Mountain to the immediate west. Sargent and Penobscot Mountains make up the bright stone ridge across the ravine to the east.

Although Parkman and Bald are not high by the standard of many other mountains in Maine, they still can be very windy. Winds from the south seem to accelerate as they come up the valley from the ocean and may often reach gale velocity on days when it's warm and calm at roadside.

To regain the road, head down on the Parkman Mountain Trail by which you ascended, using caution not to lose the trail where it crosses the carriage road.

39

Gorham and Champlain Mountains

Distance (round trip): 6 miles

Hiking time: 4 hours

Vertical rise: 1,200 feet

Maps: USGS 7½' Seal Harbor; USGS 15' Acadia National Park and Vicinity; AMC map of Mount Desert Island

Together, Gorham and Champlain Mountains form the easternmost north–south ridge on Mount Desert Island. Because their summits look down on a splendid coastline, the ridge walk is one of the best on the island. The hike here is over both peaks, from south to north, and returning.

Leave your car at the Monument Cove parking lot (indicated by a GORHAM MOUNTAIN trail sign) on Ocean Drive about 1 mile south of Sand Beach and 1 mile north of Otter Cliffs. Take the Gorham Mountain Trail, which starts on the west side of the

The cliffs of Champlain Mountain

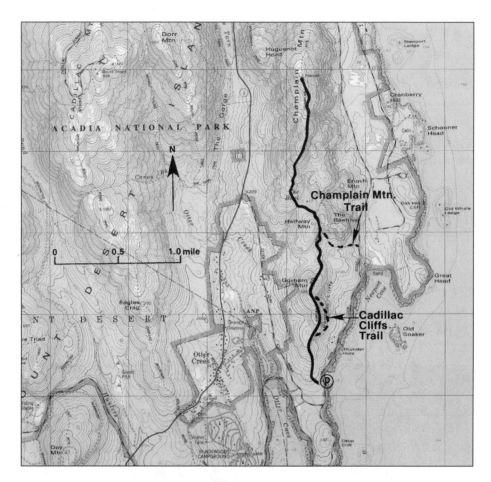

road, opposite the cove. Watch for the marker. Climb easily over open ledges for about ⅓ mile, passing the Cadillac Cliffs Loop Trail on your right. (You may take a detour for the cliffs; the loop rejoins the main trail about ⅓ mile higher up.)

Your walk above the cliffs continues, rising very slightly over open ledges with good views, passes the other end of the Cliffs Loop at about ⅔ mile, and proceeds north to the open summit at just under 1 mile. There are superb north-to-south views of the island's southeast coast here.

Over the summit, descend for ⅓ mile to a connection with the Champlain Mountain Trail. Turn northwest (left) at this junction. You ascend the south ridge of Champlain gradually, proceeding around the Bowl (a mountain tarn), which is on your right, then turn north on the open ridge with more excellent views of the ocean to the east. The summit of Champlain is reached after slightly less than 3 miles of hiking from the trailhead.

From the summit, you'll see Huguenot Head tumble northwest toward Dorr and Cadillac Mountains. The community of Bar Harbor is north-northeast from your vantage point, and Bar, Sheep Porcupine, Burnt Porcupine, and Long Porcupine Islands stand off the harbor. You will see a point of land to the southeast, above Newport Cove, which is Great Head. The long stretch of water above Bar Harbor is Frenchman Bay.

Located on this great bay, Mount Desert Island has played an intimate role in Maine's coastal history. There are signs of habitation on the island prior to 4000 B.C. The island was a favorite summer home of the Passamaquoddy and Penobscot tribes of the Abenaki nation prior to the colonial period. The Native Americans wintered at their tribal homes near Orono, Maine, paddling to the island and other coastal destinations in birchbark canoes in the warm months to fish and gather provisions.

To return via your ascent route, simply turn around on the Champlain summit and head back along the ridge and then down to where you parked.

Note: Some trail restrictions have been in effect here in recent years due to nesting peregrine falcons. Check with park headquarters to determine if restrictions are in place.

40

Penobscot and Sargent Mountains

Distance (round trip): 5 miles

Hiking time: 3½ hours

Vertical rise: 1,150 feet

Maps: USGS 15' Acadia National Park and Vicinity; AMC map of Mount Desert Island

Penobscot and Sargent Mountains form the high ridge that runs down to the west side of Jordan Pond. Leave your car at the new Jordan Pond House, a popular eating place just north of Seal Harbor on the park service road. The trail begins from the rear of the house. Watch for an arrow, indicating the trail to the west.

After a short walk from the house, cross the carriage road and bear slightly to your right over a footbridge spanning Jordan Stream. Follow signs for the Penobscot Mountain Trail. You travel west and northwest, rising very gradually for the first ⅓ mile. The trail then climbs more rapidly for a while, levels off briefly, descends to cross another brook, and turns left below a wall of granite boulders.

Slabbing left up the wall, cross a second carriage road and resume the steep northwest pitch up the ridge. The climb becomes very interesting here, and you will traverse several rock ledges that are nearly perpendicular. *Caution is required.* Be very careful not to dislodge loose rock, which could fall on a climber below. The trail here follows a series of switchbacks, with some straight vertical climbing.

After maneuvering up through a narrow crack and around another switchback, you emerge onto a ledge (right) with excellent views down to Jordan Pond and across the water to Pemetic Mountain. The two round peaks known as the Bubbles are to your left at the far end of the pond. Continue west now, climbing through a wooded area to an open ledge at the peak of the south ridge. Turn abruptly right here and head north

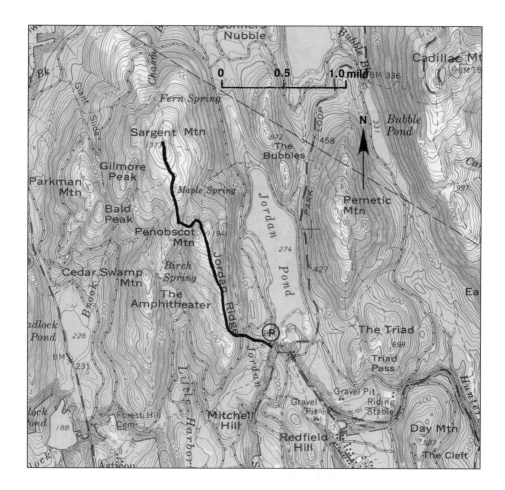

along the ridge toward the Penobscot summit.

The views are very good on the ridge (you can see almost full circle, from northeast to northwest) and get progressively better as you near the top. The trail meanders over the bare ridge, passing several false summits, and reaches the true summit, directly opposite Pemetic, at 1 ½ miles.

The summit of Sargent Mountain is just under 1 mile north. Below you to the northwest is Sargent Pond, a tiny alpine lake. To reach the pond, take the Sargent Pond Trail from the summit of Penobscot. The descent to the pond is quickly made over ledgy terrain. The South Ridge Trail is well marked and leads from the pond directly to the top of Sargent, ¾ mile farther. Allow at least an additional ½ hour to get over to Sargent.

Looking south from either peak, you will quickly come to appreciate why climbing on Mount Desert Island is unique. Besides the excellent mountain views to the west, north, and east, there are superb views of the Atlantic to the south. The point of land to the southeast is Seal Harbor, and out beyond are the islands that lie off Mount Desert's southern shores. The largest, slightly to the left, is Great Cranberry Island. To the northeast lie Little Cranberry

Penobscot Mountain over Long Pond

and Baker Islands. The three smaller islands closer to the shore are, left to right, Sutton, Bear, and Greening. Farther out, Little Duck and Great Duck may be visible if the weather is exceptionally clear. Having surveyed the peaks and islands, head down to the Jordan Pond House via the long, splendid walk south on the Penobscot Trail.

Although Penobscot and Sargent are low summits compared with Maine's major mountains, you should travel prepared. As on Cadillac and Champlain, these ridges are open to harsh wind and weather and offer little shelter. Be sure to carry extra clothing in case of sudden changes in the weather.

41

Norumbega Mountain

Distance (around loop): 2¾ miles

Hiking time: 2 hours

Vertical rise: 600 feet

Maps: USGS 15' Acadia National Park and Vicinity; AMC map of Mount Desert Island

Physically, Mount Desert Island is a heart-shaped land mass, divided in the middle by fjordlike Somes Sound, and peppered with bare summits rising dramatically from the sea. Norumbega Mountain is a low summit that forms the eastern wall of the sound and provides nearly as much good hiking as many of its higher neighbors on the mainland. The views, as one would expect, are first-class.

On its eastern perimeter, Norumbega lies side by side with Upper and Lower Hadlock Ponds. The summit, besides monitoring the length of the sound, looks south to the lowlands of Southwest Harbor and Tremont. Norumbega also forms the left leg of a horseshoe-shaped series of peaks whose eastern border consists of Sargent and Penobscot Mountains. The mountain was formerly known as Brown's Mountain after John Brown, an early settler who owned a major plot of land north of the rise.

To reach the mountain from the junction of ME 198 and ME 233, take ME 198 south along the eastern edge of Somes Sound. At 2.8 miles from the junction, watch for a parking area on the west side of the road, just above Upper Hadlock Pond.

From the parking area, walk westward on the Norumbega Mountain Trail. Ascending steeply, you turn northwestward—away from the summit—slab the ridge, and then turn south at about ⅓ mile. The climb continues southward, rising over more open granite ledges (with scattered views) and reaches the summit at ⅔ mile. The summit is wooded, but allows fine open views to the west and up the sound. The mountains

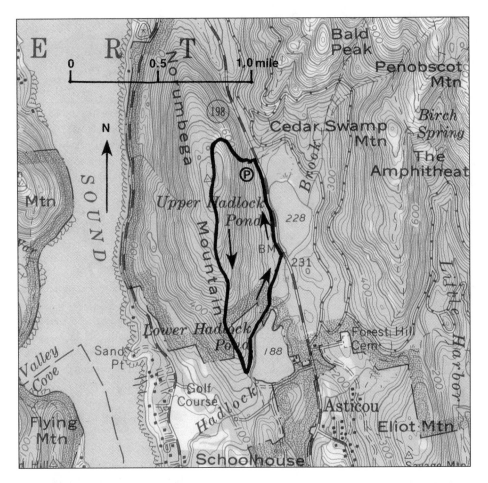

across the water are Saint Sauveur and Acadia. Farther back are Bernard, Mansell, and Beach Mountains, ranging left to right, one almost behind the other. Rest a while here and soak it all up.

There are blueberry bushes on the north ridge, and if you climb in midsummer you can gather the makings of a pie before leaving the summit. Under way again, continue down the trail to the south. The walk through mixed fir,

pine, and spruce straddles the south ridge. The trail descends easily, and about 1⅔ miles from the parking lot reaches the west shore of Lower Hadlock Pond. You turn sharply northeast here, following the *west* shore of the pond. *Keeping west* of the pond and its northern brook, you reach Route 198 at 2¼ miles. Turn left (north) on the road that takes you back to your starting point, not quite ¾ mile away.

A hiking path on Mount Desert Island

42

Acadia Mountain Loop

Distance (around loop): 2½ miles

Hiking time: 1½ hours

Vertical rise: 500 feet

Maps: USGS 7½' Southwest Harbor; USGS 15' Acadia National Park and Vicinity; AMC map of Mount Desert Island

Acadia Mountain is one of the attractive, low summits that border Somes Sound on the western half of Mount Desert Island. The sound, which many consider the only real coastal fjord in eastern America (because the mountains plunge right down to the sea here), rolls south to the sea directly under Acadia's east peak. You'll be able to approach the sound on the lower reaches of this hike where the trail crosses Man of War Brook. The area, a supremely attractive hiking ground, has many historic associations. Nearby Saint Sauveur Mountain bears the name of the early French colony on the island, founded in 1613. The colony was destroyed in a matter of weeks by marauding English coastal patrols. The English men-of-war found the deep waters of the sound a good place to drop anchor close to shore. Fresh water from Man of War Brook and fish and game from the area replenished the larders of the English fighting ships.

The west-to-east traverse of Acadia Mountain begins on ME 102, 3 miles south of Somesville and 3 miles north of Southwest Harbor. A large parking area on the west side of the road above Echo Lake is situated opposite the trailhead. The trail runs east over a bluff and into the woods. Quickly ascending a series of ledges, you walk east-southeast through groves of jack pines and birches, which are surrounded by blueberry bushes.

You shortly reach a junction, and turn north (left) through a slump overgrown with rhodora, thence climbing slightly over several ledgy ribs. In moments you cross gravel Robinson Road, reenter the woods, and di-

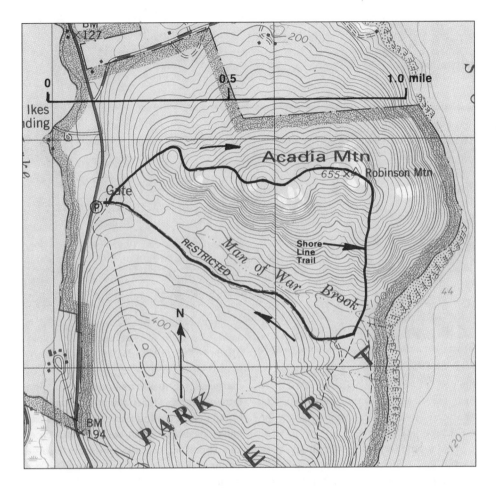

rectly ascend a low ledge. The trail now rises more steeply north-northeastward to a second ledgy area, where views to the west begin to open up. You curve around to the east-southeast over the attractive exposed granite, passing through a shady depression filled with thickly grown pine and Indian pipes. Early views of the south end of the sound may be seen here. In a few more minutes you reach Acadia's west summit, which has spectacular views to the south but is wooded on its north side. (A short side trail leads to a bald spot with good views on the north lip of the knob.) Although you'll be pleased with what you see from this spot, there are even better

views from the east peak. To get there, simply walk eastward through a depression grown up with stunted oak and rhodora, emerging on the east summit in a few minutes.

Acadia's east knob provides a splendid outlook on Somes Sound and the offshore islands to the south. Beautiful Valley Cove is below to the near south, and above it to the right lies Saint Sauveur Mountain. Flying Mountain is the low hill that juts into the water beyond the cove. Across the water, the hulk of Norumbega Mountain runs north and south. The peak to the west with the prominent tower is Beech Mountain. A number of large sailing craft are usually moored around

Acadia Mountain (right) and Norumbega Mountain over Somes Sound

the cove in fair weather. The prospect from this side of Acadia is profoundly beautiful, and you'll want to allow time to sit on the rocks here, enjoying it all.

To descend to Man of War Brook, head east of the summit over rolling ledges and down into groves of red oak. The trail turns south and makes its way over several ledges in switchbacks that are moderately steep. At ½ mile below the east peak, you enter a cedar grove and cross the brook. A link trail to your left leads 100 yards to the shoreline. Continue south on the main trail, turning

southwest (right) at a trail junction. You next cross a field and reach the end of Robinson Road. Follow the road northwest as it rises gently, passing very attractive groves of cedar. There are periodic views of the bare ledges of Acadia's west peak before you enter the woods here.

Continue along the road to the northwest for about ½ mile, watching for trail signs at the crossing. Turn left (west) at the point where you crossed the road originally, and retrace your steps to ME 102 in another ¼ mile.

43

Cadillac Mountain

Distance (round trip): 7 miles

Hiking time: 4½ hours

Vertical rise: 1,230 feet

Maps: USGS 15' Acadia National Park and Vicinity; AMC map of Mount Desert Island

Cadillac Mountain, Mount Desert's highest summit, broods over the eastern half of the island, its great 5-mile-long bulk visible from almost anywhere on the land or water around it. The mountain, named after Antoine Cadillac, who was given the island by Louis XIV in 1688, offers what is perhaps the best extended walk along open heights on the island. The walk culminates in superb views over the entire island, Frenchman Bay, and the Atlantic.

To ascend Cadillac, drive south from Bar Harbor on Route 3. Watch for trail signs on the north side of the road nearly opposite the entrance to Black Woods Campground. There is ample room to park cars on the shoulder of the road. From the road, the trail immediately enters thick woods, running north and northwest on a gradual rise through close-grown balsam, white pine, and cedar. The ground cover has been eroded in many places, and the distinctive pink granite of the island frequently protrudes.

Walk through scattered boulders and rock slabs, arriving at a junction with the loop to Eagle Crag on your right in 1 mile. Eagle Crag offers much the same views as the main trail. Keep left here and stay on the main trail under the rock outcrops, climbing northwestward to the first open ledges, with views to the southwest. At just over 1½ miles from the road, the trail wanders through birch and groves of jack pine into open, 180-degree views to the south. On summer days, a great deal of sailing activity around the islands to the south may be seen from here.

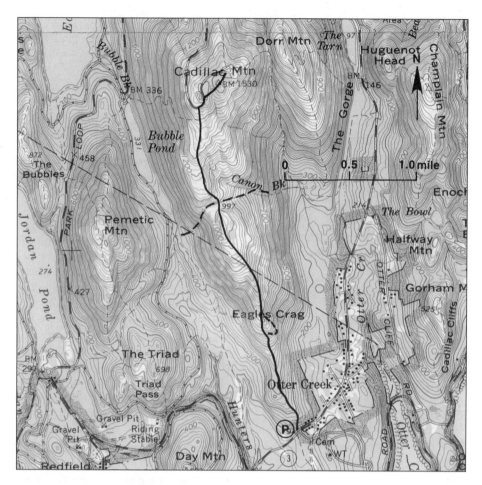

The trail continues over open ledges and through occasional scrub along the north–south rib of the mountain. Interesting dikes of metamorphosed shale are seen here and there in the rock, and the summit appears ahead to your right. You may also look east, taking in the whole range of Gorham and Champlain Mountains, including the tiny mountain tarn known as the Bowl. About 1 mile below the summit, the route descends into a gully, passing a weedy bog to your left and crossing the Canon Brook Trail.

For the remainder of the route below the summit, you walk completely in the open,

and all vegetation ceases. Winds in this area can be uncomfortable in rough weather. Continuing north-northeast across the open slab, the trail loops to the edge of the road, then runs through a wooded area to the summit over short, easy grades. In a few minutes, you pass the true summit to your left behind the service building and emerge at the summit parking area. The open ledges with the best views lie a short walk to the east.

Cadillac's summit, being the highest on the island, offers fine views in all directions. You'll see Dorr Mountain rising in the immediate foreground to the east. Behind it, the long ridge of Champlain Mountain, named

Cadillac Mountain from Somesville

after the island's discoverer, stands between Dorr and the sea. The islands in Bar
Harbor and Frenchman Bay are to the
northeast. Schoodic Point, also a part of
Acadia National Park, lies far across the
bay to the east. Pemetic, Penobscot, and
Sargent Mountains constitute the most imposing summits to the west, and are best
seen in their entirety from the summit's
west parking area.

From up here, it isn't hard to see why
Mount Desert became such a hotly contested prize among the early colonial set-
tlers. Discovered and first colonized by the
French, the island later passed into British
hands before being taken by the American
colonials. Its abundant excellent harbors,
game, and notable water supplies made it a
treasure worth pursuing as a base for con-
trolling the surrounding waters .

To return to your car at Black Woods,
retrace your route downward. The walk
from the 1,500-foot summit to ME 3 can be
done in less than 2 hours.

44

Sand Beach and Great Head

Distance (round trip): 2 miles

Hiking time: 1½ hours

Vertical rise: 200 feet

Maps: USGS 7½' Seal Harbor; USGS 15' Acadia National Park and Vicinity; AMC map of Mount Desert Island

One of the most attractive stretches of shoreline on Mount Desert Island, Sand Beach and Great Head provide the walker with an easy route through varied, always beautiful terrain. The Head itself gives the hiker access to what are probably the best shoreline views on the east side of the island across the water to the Schoodic Peninsula. And since the elevation gains on this route are minor, it's a good walk with youngsters or an undemanding stroll on a day when you'd like to mosey along the shore, avoiding the steeper climbs of Mount Desert's higher summits.

From Bar Harbor, head south on ME 3, reaching a fork in the road about 1 mile from the center of town. Keep to the left here on Schooner Head Road. Stay on this road for about 3 miles, making no turns, until it terminates at a barrier. Turn around here and park in the new parking lot at the trailhead, which is marked by a wooden pillar about 200 yards before the road ends.

This walk makes a loop past Sand Beach and offers a shorter return over the inland ledges of the head, or a longer walk along the perimeter of the head, rejoining the shorter loop on the return. Both walks are undemanding and, except for a brief scramble up the ledges, require little climbing.

Begin by walking south on the trail through white birch, steeplebush, and spruce. The route lies over a broad woods road now turned grassy and well shaded. In a few hundred feet, you will pass the return leg of the path coming in on your left. Proceed straight ahead, and reach the bluffs over Sand Beach in ½ mile. Spectacular views over the beach

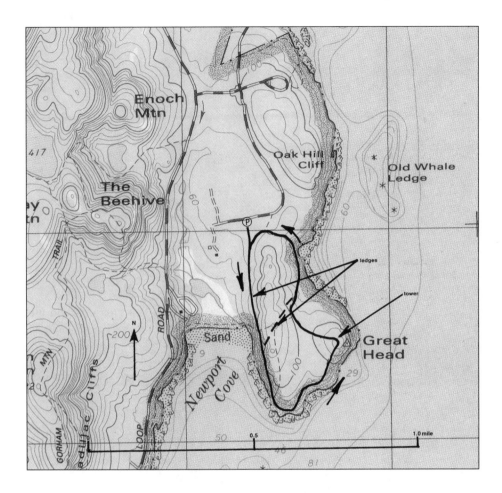

and up to the Beehive, a rounded granitic mountain, open up to the west. You may wish to descend to the beach via a pathway now and explore the shore and the pretty freshwater lagoon behind it. Herons, ducks, and other shorebirds are often seen, particularly in early morning. The beach itself is a fine expanse of yellow sand that caps Newport Cove. Visit here in early or late season if you can. In high summer, the crowds descend.

Opposite the point where the side trail descends to the beach, the shorter of the two loops zigzags directly up a ledge marked with red blazes. If you wish to re-turn this way, head up the ledge and arrive at a bare summit with superb views to the east and back to the west over the Beehive and Champlain Mountain. The route then descends from the ledges and loops back on a well-marked trail to the junction mentioned earlier.

To reach Great Head, continue south and southeast, gradually rounding the end of the peninsula over mossy ground and rising and falling through aspen and birch. Following the red blazes and, later, cairns, you arrive shortly at the ruined stone tower near Great Head's 145-foot, precipitous drop to the broad Atlantic. You can see in

Sand Beach

all directions here: back to the mountains of the island, southeast to the open ocean, to the east across Frenchman Bay to the Schoodic region, and northeast to the mountains of the mainland. The squarish building on the tiny island is Egg Rock lighthouse, a beacon for the considerable water traffic that moves up and down the bay. Around to the southwest are the high, dark ledges forming Otter Cliffs. From here, you can also see the Beehive and Champlain Mountain again, along whose summit ridges there are excellent, long, north–south day hikes (see Hike 39).

To return, leave the tower site and walk northwest, descending soon to a boggy area over more ledge. Scattered alders, bracken fern, and occasional spruce line the path as you move within earshot of the shore. Just beyond a thick stand of young birch where the ground is carpeted with bunchberry, Canada mayflower, moss, and lichen, you join the shorter of the two loop trails as it comes in on your left. Continuing northwest over easy grades, the trail broadens and becomes less stony. Reaching a height-of-land in a small clearing, descend slightly, curving more westerly, and soon reach the main trail on which you began the walk. Bear right (north) here, and you'll gain the paved road and your parking place in just a few minutes.

This walk can also be done in milder winters when there is likely to be little snow cover on the island. Good hiking boots should always be worn in winter and during inclement weather, as the frequent ledge-walking on this hike can be slippery.

Mount Desert Island–Acadia National Park

45

The Bubbles

Distance (round trip): 3½ miles

Hiking time: 2 hours

Vertical rise: 800 feet

Maps: USGS 15' Acadia National Park and Vicinity; AMC map of Mount Desert Island

The Bubbles are two 800-foot mounds of pink granite that dominate the northern end of Jordan Pond in the east-central portion of Mount Desert Island. The sister mountains form a striking profile that at first may discourage the hiker with no technical climbing experience. In fact, these two very rocky peaks require no special mountaineering skills and are readily accessible to the average hiker. The Bubbles not only offer a challenging outing for the hiker, but they also are an elegant platform in the midst of Acadia National Park for viewing nearly all of the major summits that surround it.

This hike is directly reached by driving ME 3 east from Ellsworth to the north end of Mount Desert Island and turning onto the park service road at the Hulls Cove entrance. An information center is just inside this entrance; ask for directions and park maps here if you need them. Proceed south on the park service road to the Bubble Rock parking area north of Jordan Pond. This spot is also known as the "Bubble-Pemetic" parking area, and shouldn't be confused with the "Bubbles" parking lot still another half mile farther south.

The walk begins to the west from the parking area, rising up through closely grown beech, birch, and striped maple. You reach a junction in less than ⅛ mile and cross the Jordan Pond Carry Trail. From here, continue straight on up an old tote road, bearing gradually to the left, over several water bars, arriving shortly at another junction. Trails lead from this junction to both of the Bubble summits.

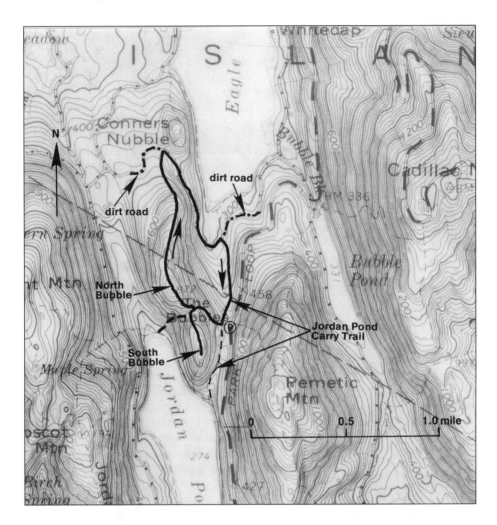

Bear left and ascend the trail to the South Bubble. The climb is brisk up through young beech and birch. With Pemetic Mountain off to your left, you keep left at the junction with the trail from Jordan Pond. Views to the North Bubble begin to open up behind you now. At just under 800 feet, the summit of the South Bubble is an open expanse of glacier-scarred granite, onto which you soon emerge after a final march amid scraggly birch and alder.

Potassium feldspar accounts for the characteristic pink glow of Mount Desert's coarse granite hills. The igneous stone was formed approximately 350 million years ago and has been glacially scoured several times since, most recently 18,000 to 11,000 years ago. The Laurentide ice sheet, the most recent of the glacial waves to come down from the northwest over New England, was roughly 5,000 feet thick as it built up and then slid over this range. One effect of the ice was the pleasing, rounded shape of the mountains in this area, further aided by subsequent weathering. As the ice moved through any depres-

Mount Desert Island–Acadia National Park

North Bubble (right) and Pemetic Mountain over Eagle Lake

sions, it ground and chiseled them until they became the valleys that run characteristically north and south on Mount Desert.

The north and northwest sides of most mountains in Acadia bear glacial scars from the grinding, rolling action of stone and sand carried along by glacial ice. As the ice moved over these ranges, the mobile sand and stone were dragged under tremendous pressure across existing formations. Those mountains' southern and southeastern sides of Mount Desert show rather sheer, precipitous faces due to the circular motion of glacially carried rock known as "plucking." Both of the Bubbles exhibit scarring and plucking.

Jordan and Great Ponds give you a sense of how efficient glacial action could be at scraping off deposits and carrying them away. The ponds are quite deep from the scouring and transporting action of sheet ice. The material dredged from these spots by the action of the ice was deposited farther down at the south ends of the valleys. The action of the great ice sheets also transported large boulders, called glacial erratics, from distances as great as 20 miles. One of the most prominent of these erratics can be seen just a few yards south of the South Bubble summit.

When you've had a chance to look around at the surrounding hills, descend to the junction with the North Bubble Trail, turning left and beginning the walk up the second peak. The route is to the north through more dwarf birch and over ledge with Pemetic and Cadillac Mountains in striking profile to the east and northeast. You shortly pass several cairns and proceed over the creased granite mentioned earlier. Mountain cranberries lie beneath a corridor of young pitch pines and red spruces as you walk on the summit of North Bubble.

From this second peak, a beautiful view of Eagle Lake to the north greets you. Beyond it farther to the northeast is the great expanse of Frenchman Bay. Off to the west is the long massif of Penobscot and Sargent

The Bubbles

Mountains. This more northerly of the two Bubbles is the higher at nearly 900 feet, and from it you can look back over the route you've followed thus far, and also ahead to the route down to the north along the ridge toward Conners Nubble and Eagle Lake.

Head down the open ridge, which supports little growth, having been burned over in the great Bar Harbor fires of 1947. Follow the cairns down the ledges, enjoying the continuing views of Cadillac, Acadia's highest mountain, as you proceed northward. A little more than ¾ mile below the north summit, you reach a carriage trail. Bear right and east here and walk another ¾ mile downhill into the woods until you reach the Jordan Pond Carry Trail. Turn right here onto this sometimes wet, boggy trail and ascend slowly through beech and hemlock groves to the first trail junction of this hike. At the junction, go left and you'll regain the parking area in a couple of minutes.

46

Saint Sauveur–Flying Mountain Loop

Distance (round trip): 6 miles

Hiking time: 3 hours

Vertical rise: 1,100 feet

Maps: USGS 7½' Southwest Harbor; USGS 15' Acadia National Park and Vicinity; AMC map of Mount Desert Island

For fine views over the narrows at the south end of magnificent Somes Sound, the circle over Saint Sauveur and Flying Mountains near Southwest Harbor makes an excellent walk. This route takes the hiker over three low summits in the less-frequented quarter of Mount Desert Island. The walk is both prettily wooded in sections and also barren, ledgy, and open in places, providing a platform that looks seaward. And because Saint Sauveur lies in an area off the beaten tourist path, you can walk here with relative privacy even in high summer.

The hike begins at the same spot as the Acadia Mountain loop (see Hike 42) on ME 102, 3 miles south of Somesville and 3 miles north of Southwest Harbor. The parking area on ME 102 is well marked and easy to find directly across from the trailhead. There are some fine outlooks over Echo Lake, too, as you drive south from Somesville.

Enter the woods headed eastward on the Acadia Mountain Trail and follow this path for just a short distance before reaching the Saint Sauveur Trail on your right. Bear right here and begin the straightforward march to the southeast up the northwest flanks of Saint Sauveur. These are pretty woods, characterized by abundant Scotch pine, gray birch, and other young hardwoods. Crossing a seasonal brook and passing through several clearings, you rise gradually toward the summit with views of Acadia Mountain opening up behind you. One mile from your starting place, you pass the Ledge Trail on your right. Continue southeast another ⅓ mile, now out in the open, to the bare, ledgy summit of Saint Sauveur.

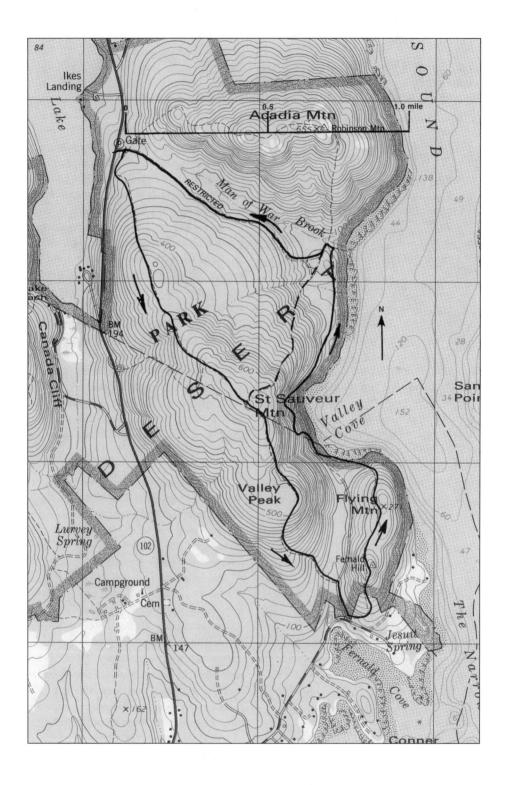

The mountain takes its name from the ill-fated French settlement established here by the Jesuits in 1613. The French mission had set out for Bangor but was blown into Frenchman Bay by a severe storm. After exploring the south coast of the island, the lower reaches of Somes Sound seemed a good place to establish a base, particularly with fresh water available in nearby Man of War Brook. However, in just weeks the colony was discovered by the patrolling English frigate *Treasurer* under the command of Samuel Argall.

James I of England claimed Mount Desert's shores during this period, and the mandate of English coasters was to put short shrift to any French attempts to develop permanent settlements here. In full battle dress, the *Treasurer* bore down on the French ship *Jonas,* moored off Fernald Cove below Flying Mountain. The French were quite unprepared for the arrival of an English 14-gunner, and fled into the woods of Saint Sauveur. Members of the short-lived colony surrendered to the British the next day. A full and colorful description of this and other military and naval actions can be found in Samuel Eliot Morison's *The Story of Mount Desert Island,* available in many shops in Bar Harbor and Ellsworth.

Saint Sauveur's summit ledges are surrounded by low spruce, so the views are less good here than on the ridge you've just come up and farther along in this hike. Proceed off the summit to Eagle Cliffs, a far better outlook, just past a clearing laced with juniper bushes. The panorama of Somes Sound, spreading itself out beneath you, is magnificent, and you'll probably want to rest here a while and enjoy watching the movement of boats up and down the sound. Valley Cove is the rounded bay immediately to the east.

From Eagle Cliffs, take the left trail at a junction and descend gradually to Valley Peak through juniper and blueberry bushes. Valley Peak, an arm of Saint Sauveur Mountain, offers additional opportunities to see the ocean and the sound as you proceed southeastward. Moving through cedar and spruce cover, you walk over heavily gouged granite ledge and onto Valley Peak's 520-foot summit.

The trail next pulls around to the west, providing good views of Fernald Cove and Southwest Harbor. Gnarled oaks and white pines border the path as you descend nearly to sea level. You walk through a cedar bog and over two plank bridges, emerging in minutes on a gravel right-of-way known as Valley Cove Truck Road. Head right on the road for 100 yards, and then bear left on Flying Mountain Trail, which is clearly marked. Making the turn here, you're at the most southerly point on the walk.

The walk takes you uphill again through columns of tall cedars on Flying Mountain's south arm. Very shortly you arrive on the ledgy summit. Valley Peak, Beech, and Mansell Mountains are off to the northwest. The pot shape of Greening Island floats to the southeast off Southwest Harbor. Fernald Cove is directly below you to the south. Although Flying Mountain is the lowest of the three moderate summits in this loop, you have the feeling of being up high here because of the abrupt rise of these hills from the water.

Resuming the hike, you'll bear around to the east looking out over the narrows. If you happen to hit this spot at low tide, you'll note that Somes Sound is nearly a lake at such moments, given the shallow bar at the narrows. You now descend fairly steeply for 1/3 mile to Valley Cove. On a warm summer day, you may want to picnic here and have a swim. To get on the beach, leave the trail where it crosses a footbridge near the shore. Valley Cove Spring signs appear

The hills of Mount Desert overlooking Southwest Harbor

momentarily. This *may* be a source of water, but is unpredictable.

Skirting the cove, proceed through a collection of boulders where polypody fern, rock tripe, and moss grow. Cross a slide and ascend a series of stone steps as you move north of the cove. Eagle Cliffs hangs above you to the left on Saint Sauveur. Continuing northward, cross another slide, which requires caution, and pick up the trail again on its other side. The trail then drops to the water's edge and enters the woods.

After a short walk along the shore of the sound, enter a cedar bog and come to Man of War Brook. Watch for a woods road on your left, and turn west here. This is the same route back to the highway that one takes when completing the Acadia Mountain loop. From here, walk through a field and you'll reach the end of Robinson Road in a few hundred yards. You then continue to the northwest through groves of cedar and, staying with the trail, reach ME 102 and your car in about ½ mile.

47

Beech Mountain

Distance (around loop): 3½ miles

Hiking time: 2½ hours

Vertical rise: 700 feet

Maps: USGS 7½' Southwest Harbor; USGS 15' Acadia National Park and Vicinity; AMC map of Mount Desert Island

Beech Mountain, one of a circle of low hills in the remote western quarter of Mount Desert Island, is notable for its unspoiled beauty. Situated on the little-traveled west side of Echo Lake, Beech Mountain is the highest point on a long ridge separating Echo Lake and the much larger Long Pond. A variety of paths winds around the mountain through attractive woods, boulder gardens, and splendid, open ledges. Except for the initial gain in altitude, the trail is not difficult or demanding. Even a beginning hiker will find this an easy and very pleasant walk.

To reach the mountain, follow ME 3 south and east from Ellsworth to its junction with ME 102 and ME 198 just beyond the Thompson Island Information Center as you enter Mount Desert Island. Bear right and follow ME 102 to Somesville. From the center of this little village, bear right ⅓ mile past Higgins Market and continue on ME 102 as it heads west. In less than ¼ mile you bear left onto Beech Hill Road. The road runs south along a high ridge, gradually leaves the houses behind, and rolls toward Beech Mountain. Pretty, open fields, grown thick with low-bush blueberries, yield fine views to Beech and to Bernard and Mansell Mountains to the southwest and to other ranges on the island off to the east.

Beech Hill Road ends abruptly at a parking lot just over 3 miles from its junction with ME 102. Park to the right under the cliffs. Take the trail that leaves the northwest corner of the parking area. This trail moves upward to the west for several hundred yards before coming to a trail junction.

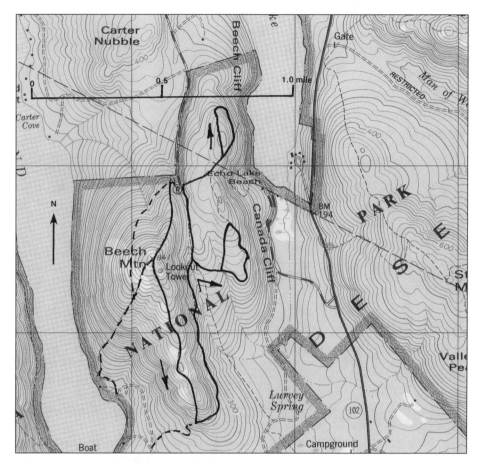

Keep to the left at the junction and take the higher of two trails to the summit. On this route, you shortly move onto open ledge with excellent outlooks back to the north over Echo Lake and to Somesville, with its prominent white church steeple. Good views across Somes Sound to Norumbega and Penobscot Mountains are found here. In less than ½ mile from the parking lot, you arrive at the convergence of the two trails at the observation tower on Beech's 839-foot summit.

Beech's summit plateau, overgrown with sheep laurel, provides 360-degree views including those to the south toward Greening Island, the Cranberry Isles, and the Atlantic. Mansell and Bernard Mountains loom to the southwest across the southern neck of Long Pond. The pond, a beautiful, slim expanse of water running north and south, is the largest landlocked body of water on Mount Desert.

To continue beyond the summit, take the South Ridge Trail toward the ocean, descending a granite ridge dotted with lichen. The route is alternately in the open and in the woods. You are as likely as not to see deer tracks along here. British soldiers—tiny, red-capped lichens—cranberries, gray-green reindeer lichen, and heather grow among the rocks. Reaching a set of stone steps, take a sharp left downhill. The open

Long Pond

ledges now give way to shady bowers of spruce. A series of switchbacks descends through mossy cascades and thick groves of birch and beech, bringing you to a junction with a side trail that runs to Long Pond. Instead, bear left onto the Valley Trail, heading away from the pond. Walk due north on the Valley Trail, passing through varied growth and past a jumble of granite slabs stacked here long ago by glacial movement. This ancient stonework is now covered with polypody fern and a foliose lichen known as rock tripe.

From where you made the turn onto the Valley Trail to the parking area is just under 1 mile. Approximately ⅔ mile along this path, you come to the Canada Cliffs Loop Trail on your right. Turn right (east) here at the sign, cross a boggy area, climb a brief rise, and then walk down through a cedar bog on a series of plank bridges. This trail shortly forks, each side being the "leg" of a loop over the cliffs. Keep right and you'll soon be on the ledges with fine views east

to Saint Sauveur Mountain. The other leg of the trail comes in about 50 yards from the summit. Make a mental note of this spot, as you'll return on the other leg on your way back to the Valley Trail. A walk of a few more yards brings you to the high point on these dramatic, open cliffs with excellent outlooks to Echo Lake and the northeast. Picking up the other leg of the loop, proceed briefly west to the Valley Trail, and then turn northward (right) toward your starting place.

If, when you reach the parking lot, you've still some energy left, another short loop runs off to the northeast over Beech Cliff. Look for the sign that indicates this loop across the road opposite the northeast corner of the parking lot. Keep left just past the sign and make the short walk (about ⅓ mile) through groves of spruce and cedar eastward to Beech Cliff over Echo Lake. The views over Echo Lake are even better than those you experienced on Canada Cliffs. The granite here bears the familiar

---

Beech Mountain   203

scouring of glacial activity so common on the summits of Mount Desert.

After passing over the top point of this cliff, bear around to the south on a lower trail, gradually pulling west and rejoining the short leg to the parking lot. On this lower, return loop, you come around again to the fork where you stayed left on the way in. A third trail here makes a rise over a hill and then descends gradually through a series of ladders and switchbacks to Echo Lake. The walk down this trail to the water is about a ¾-mile round trip. (The trail to the water isn't included in the time and distance estimates at the top of this hike description.)

VIII

Eastern Maine: The "Air Line" and the Eastern Maine Coast

48

Great Pond Mountain

Distance (round trip): 4¼ miles

Hiking time: 2½ hours

Vertical rise: 650 feet

Map: USGS 15' Orland

Great Pond Mountain, sometimes referred to as "Great Hill," tends to be a locals' mountain, the source of a perfect hike never overrun by the hordes who race hell-bent for the more famous hills of Mount Desert to the east. Largely undiscovered, well hidden back in the woods to the north of US 1 in Orland, Great Pond Mountain provides a relaxed, beautiful walk in quiet surroundings reminiscent of a Maine less traveled. The route rewards the hiker with exceptional views without much vertical scrambling, and it's easy enough to bring youngsters along without complaint. In short, you'll find this a great family hike with only positive surprises.

The mountain is approached from US 1 on a side road that leaves the main highway at a point 1½ miles east of the junction of US 1 and ME 15 in Orland (6 miles east of the center of Bucksport). Turn north onto the side road, signed CRAIG BROOK NATIONAL FISH HATCHERY, and follow this road, which is first paved and then gravel, westward to the hatchery grounds. Park by the visitors center.

If this is a first visit, you may wish to spend some time exploring the Craig Brook Hatchery grounds before setting out. You are on the site of America's oldest salmon hatchery, established in 1871. The hatchery raceways and display pool are visible on the hillside, which drops toward Alamoosook Lake. The visitors center provides interesting displays and information on the propagation and research done at this facility, which began with the work of Dr. Charles Atkins in the late 1860s.

The trail to Great Pond Mountain leaves

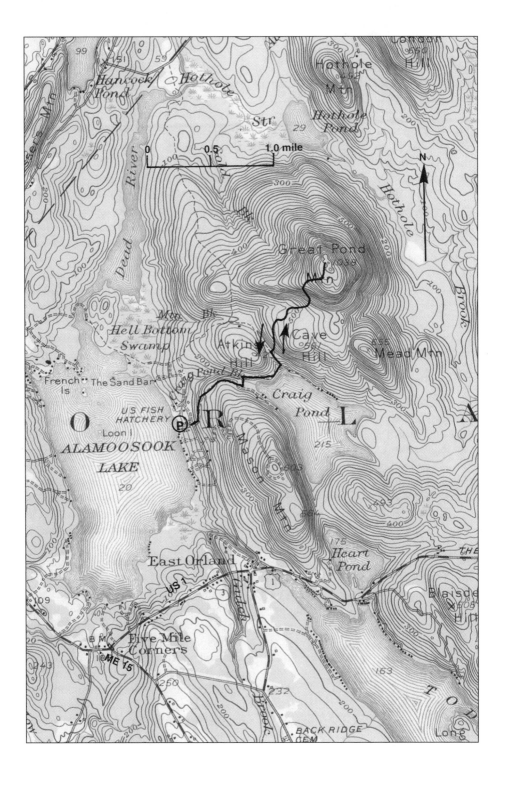

the notice board by the visitors center and runs west for a moment along the road, making an immediate turn around some buildings to the right (north). Follow this pleasant, shady, gravel road as it meanders northward toward 200-acre Craig Pond. In about ½ mile, you pass a grassy turnout to your right where a nature trail makes a 1-mile scenic loop through the Craig Brook area. Continuing northward, stay on the main gravel road, passing several roads or paths that drift off into the woods. Just over a mile from your starting point and just before you reach the Craig Pond gate, look for a very rough gravel road that forks to your left. Here you begin the uphill tramp to the ledgy summit of Great Pond Mountain. Head up the gravel side road; it's scoured and uneven and becomes a streamed in wet weather. You'll pass a message box, placed by the Great Pond Mountain Conservation Trust, on a tree to your right. Follow the road west and northwest. Wild raspberries, goldenrod, and dense brush border the road. This land appears to have been logged over about a decade or so ago. Pass a side road to your left, and continue uphill briskly through young beech and ash.

The road rises quickly, and scattered hemlocks appear. Sections of fractured and weathered granodioritic rock lie in the roadbed. As you proceed, this rock becomes fully exposed, giving the road an almost paved look. The route pulls around to your right (north) by a small cairn, passing a grassy road that departs to your left. Coniferous trees begin to grow in greater density here, with white pine, red spruce, and balsam evident. The air carries their pleasing fragrance.

Running through a clearing, the road re-enters a wooded area and, climbing gradually, pulls around toward the east and northeast. The land to the west begins to drop away, and you have a sense of gaining altitude. The road crosses bands of ledge, returning here and there to gravel and narrowing to a path in places. The exposed ledge gives a hint of its formation in a molten state, millions of years ago, and seems to flow downward in frozen waves. You can also see how thin the topsoil is here over the great stone underlayment, yet grasses and trees manage to hold on.

The road divides briefly around a little island of trees at a tall hemlock. Going east and northeast, pass a grove of older hemlock; beech and white birch appear. Soon you walk into a more open area, where the route turns northward. White oak and pine border a grassy verge. Some views over Alamoosook Lake open to the south. Ground blueberries grow plentifully to the left of the trail.

The summit ledges become visible higher up and to the north. Dotted with lichen-crusted rock, this spot has a pleasant, open feel to it. Birch, spruce, balsam, and more oak lie along the way. Haircap and sphagnum mosses are visible. Keep your eyes open, too, for a little side trail on your left through stands of evergreens. A few steps off the main route here will bring you to good early views to the southwest and west. If you cross the main trail and walk eastward, there are also fine views to the east and southeast. You can, in fact, easily see all the way to the Atlantic on a clear day.

At the top of this long, open rise the trail turns sharply left and then right again, rising farther through dense evergreens. It is interesting to see how closely the climatic zones are layered on this little mountain. In this colder elevation, you have left the deciduous growth mostly behind. You shortly pass a road that comes in on your left. (Remember this point, and remember to bear *left* at this junction on your descent.) A series of open, ledgy clearings alternates with sections where spruce and hemlock crowd

Ridge Trail at Great Pond Mountain

the path. Bunchberries, scattered ferns, white pines, and birches border the way.

You now climb the final rise to the summit ledges. The route turns abruptly right, then left, arriving on the more or less flat and open summit, a great pancake of granitic ledge. (The true summit, only slightly higher and more wooded, is through the grove of evergreens to the north.) Before you are 180-degree outlooks over some of Maine's most handsome coastal terrain. The numerous peaks of Mount Desert lie to the east, south of prominent Schoodic Mountain. The distinctive, conelike lump of Blue Hill is to the southeast. Mount Waldo rises around to the west on the other side of Bucksport. Branch, Green, and Graham Lakes are in the valleys to the east. Almost

anywhere on these rangy ledges makes a good picnic spot, and you aren't likely to be disturbed by many visitors even at the height of the summer season.

Although Great Pond Mountain is a pleasant climb year-round, it's superb in foliage season, both for its broad views over much forestland and for the colorful, mixed vegetation along its own path. The experienced snowshoer or hiker with crampons will find it an excellent and challenging winter walk, too.

To regain your starting point, carefully retrace your steps down the mountain and southward on the access road, being careful not to leave the main route on any of the numerous side roads and trails that head off in various directions.

49

Peaked Mountain (Chick Hill)

Distance (round trip): 2½ miles

Hiking time: 1½ hours

Vertical rise: 800 feet

Map: USGS 15' Great Pond

Peaked Mountain, known locally as Chick Hill, is found in the center of Hancock County, about 18 miles east of Bangor on the Air Line (ME 9) between Clifton and Amherst. This low mountain with two open, ledgy summits offers a striking profile to travelers on ME 9, particularly those approaching from the west. An abandoned, 40-foot fire tower on the higher of the two summits affords an exceptional vantage point over what is largely wild, unspoiled country.

The mountain can be reached by driving east from Bangor on ME 9 and looking left for the access road 12.5 miles east of the junction of ME 9 and ME 178 in Eddington. If you arrive from the east, turn right on the access road 3.5 miles west of the junction of ME 9 and ME 180 in Clifton. This side road is known as Chick Hill Road, but the sign is not right on ME 9, but up the side road about 100 feet, mounted high on a utility pole. This turn is easily located by watching for a FIRE ROAD 31 sign facing west on ME 9.

Turning north on Chick Hill Road, you shortly run out of pavement. Continue around the bend and uphill to your right on a gravel surface past several houses and mobile homes. You'll be able to see the mountain on your right. In barely 0.5 mile, the road forks. Park off the right-of-way here.

The trail, an old carriage road that used to be a link in the Air Line many years ago, has grown over with tall grass and is sheltered by dense mixed growth. Walk up this steep woods road to the northeast, pass-

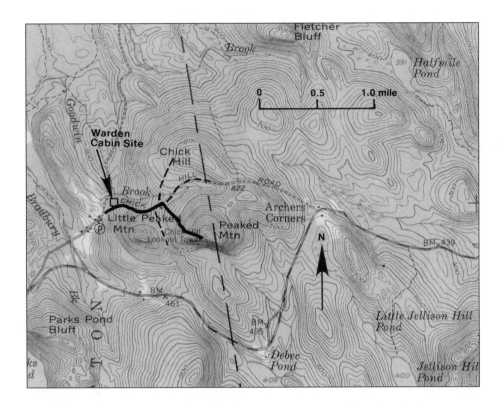

ing the old warden's cabin site in about ¼ mile. A spring-fed brook here is the last water on this hike. Jack-in-the-pulpits, fireweed, and several varieties of fern bloom along the trail here in spring and summer.

Soon you pass a grassy tote road on your right and fork to the left at ½ mile from where you parked. The trail levels off some just beyond this section, and then bears right off the old road you've been following and onto a smaller woods road designated by old ax blazes. Here and there the downed line of the warden's telephone may be seen. You next climb gradually through stands of maple, young oak, and striped maple.

The trail begins a sharp rise at just under 1 mile. As you begin this steeper ascent, you will see Little Peaked Mountain to your right. It is the westernmost of the three summits that are lumped together as "Chick Hill." This summit is trailless, but it can be climbed by bushwhacking southwest from the col between it and Peaked Mountain, your destination. The best views lie ahead on the higher summit, however.

You continue southeastward now on the steep rise to Peaked Mountain (referred to locally as "Big Chick"), shortly arriving on the open ledges marked by several cairns. Your route here runs over coarse granite. The top of Little Peaked Mountain becomes visible at your back. The eroded rock path soon brings you to the summit of Peaked Mountain and the disused warden's tower. Scattered blueberry patches dot the summit.

The 1,160-foot summit provides 360-degree views over Hancock County and

Peaked Mountain from the "Air Line"

east into Washington County. Chemo Pond and the Penobscot River are to your west over Little Peaked. Far to the northwest you may see Katahdin if the weather is clear. Chick Hill, whose name has been generalized to all three summits, is the small knob to the immediate north. Saddleback Mountain, Fletcher Bluff, and Bald Mountain are prominent peaks to the northeast in Amherst. Lead Mountain lies far off to the east. Bradbury Brook divides a marsh to the southeast across the road. Some of the major summits of Acadia National Park on Mount Desert Island show up to the south if hazy skies don't obscure them. Debec and Hopkins Ponds rest immediately below to the south.

The walk back to your car retraces the route of the ascent. You may want to make the side trip to Little Peaked Mountain on your way down. Use caution on the exposed, ledgy areas of both mountains.

50

Cutler Coastal Trail Circuit

Distance (around circuit): 5½ miles

Hiking time: 4 hours

Vertical rise: 400 feet

Maps: USGS 7½' Cutler

Away *downeast* lies a hikers' preserve that will delight anyone drawn to those precincts where land and ocean merge in dramatic surroundings. The Cutler Coastal Trail offers a demanding, interesting, truly spectacular tramp along eastern Maine's border with the Atlantic, providing hikers with access to ocean views rivaling those of California's Big Sur. Great sea cliffs, rolling surf, unspoiled heathlands, and constantly varying terrain are all a part of this quiet and little-visited route.

The Cutler Coastal Trail is also an excellent example of cooperative efforts among government agencies, preservation organizations, and conservation teams to protect a key natural area and to adapt it sensitively for recreational use. Acquired by Land for Maine's Future and developed with the guidance of the Bureau of Public Lands in the Maine Department of Conservation, construction of the Cutler Coastal Trail has involved the efforts of the College Conservation Corps of Maine, the Maine Conservation Corps, the Maine Coast Heritage Trust, wildlife biologists, recreation specialists, and regional foresters. The result is the longest coastal trail in Maine and, certainly, one of the most beautiful on the Eastern Seaboard.

To reach the trailhead, drive south from US 1 in Machias on ME 191 to the village of Cutler. Staying on ME 191, drive 3.8 miles north of the Cutler post office, and locate the trail marker on your right at the edge of an attractive heath. When you've found the trailhead, drive another 100 yards farther north and park in a small gravel lot on the

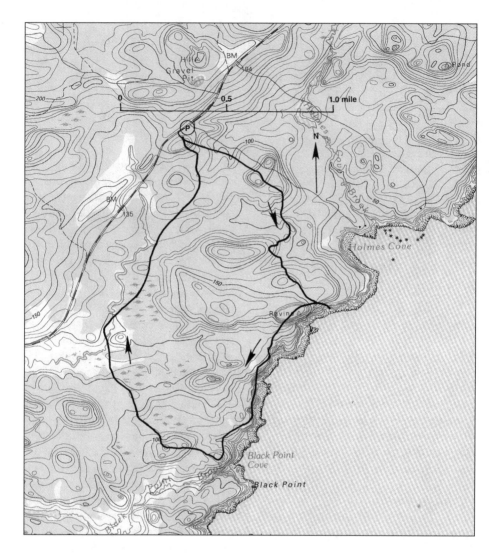

right-hand side of the road. Walk back to the trailhead when you're ready to hike.

From the trail signboard, the path runs across the heath, dividing immediately, with one route heading around to the south and the other—the one you'll follow—heading more or less straight southeastward into the woods. This left path runs along a nearly obliterated Jeep track in the tall grass toward some birches and tamaracks. Entering the woods on what shortly becomes a grown-up old woods road, the blue-blazed trail meanders generally eastward in stands of red and white spruce and northern white cedar. Eye-catching patches of green *Sphagnum centrale* and *Sphagnum gergensonii* are interlaced with equally abundant plots of haircap moss. Clumps of rhodora and ground blueberries lie on both sides of the path.

The trail is easily followed through dense growth to the east-northeast. Open

Cutler Harbor

spots interrupt the close-grown cover from time to time. Stands of birch and alder grow amid the dominant white spruce. You shortly reach a long, straight corridor, at the end of which brush blocks the road; bear right on the blue-blazed trail to the southeast. After turning, you pass the first of several cedar groves in this section of the hike and walk through a clearing. Patches of reindeer lichen grow here and there.

The trail wanders southeast and south through a dense white spruce bog and passes two low granite outcrops. Some older, taller stands of trees are passed. Farther along, you come to another broad cedar grove traversed by a boardwalk. Unharvested cedar bogs of this type are increasingly rare, and it's worth a stop here to take in this exceptional forest. The trail now works its way continuously southeast and south through more spruce, birch, and balsam, intersects with other tote roads, and eventually arrives, running easterly, in more open terrain occupied by sumac growth. You'll hear the sound of the ocean

soon and emerge, in a few more minutes, on the cliffs high above the Atlantic.

The superb outlooks here are just the first of dozens that exist in the next 2 miles as the trail follows the clifftops southwestward. The trail climbs northwest to reach higher ground, then pulls around to your left to cling to the heights above the cliffs once again. You walk over uneven terrain, with the trail climbing onto a higher vantage point one minute and then dropping closer to the surf the next. Cutting inland momentarily, the trail will quickly reverse itself and cross some high, vertiginous spots over the ledges. You'll probably never gain or lose more than 50 feet of elevation in any one part of this precipice walk, but the cumulative effect of so much up and down work is rather like climbing a 800-foot hill before day's end. The route in this section skirts a series of plunging cliffs. Use great caution, especially in wet weather.

Working your way southward, you skirt several coves, cross some grassy heathland, and clamber over fractured seaward ledge before reaching Black Point. Here there are impressive outlooks back northeast to the headlands along which you just walked. The route now leaves these spectacular cliffs and begins an interesting walk into the interior. (A further extension of this oceanside trail will allow hikers to continue to Ferry Head, returning west and north from there on another trail. Check with the Maine Bureau of Public Lands for the latest information on this trail work. The extension will add approximately 4 miles to the loop described here.)

Traveling west and northwest, the return trail gradually progresses inland over several rock ribs, rising gently but steadily through scattered hardwoods. There are good views across the heath in many places. Meandering for a while through tall swale, the trail often dips in and out of more stands of the area's characteristic white spruce and pulls steadily northward. Blue blazes on ledgy outcrops mark the route. The trail here is well groomed and easy to follow. Traversing a series of small, grassy hummocks, the path pulls finally to the northwest, crosses the open heath, and arrives at the roadside trailhead once again. Walk the paved road the short distance to your car.

Safety note: Hikers who bring children with them on any part of this route should be aware that the author's references to unprotected precipices high over ledge and open ocean are not exaggerated. For the careless, the danger of long falls onto ledge or into deep waters with treacherous currents is real. This hike is one of the most beautiful of its kind in eastern America, but all trail users should walk with caution when near the cliffs.

The Maine Bureau of Public Lands has planned for the creation of a small, primitive, hike-in camping area within this trail network. Hikers seeking more information about low-impact camping possibilities here should contact Steve Spencer at the Maine Bureau of Public Lands, State House Station 22, Augusta 04333.

Index

M

N

O

P

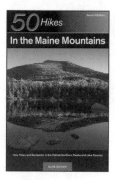
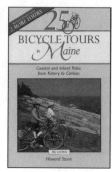
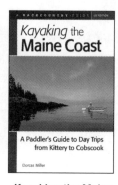
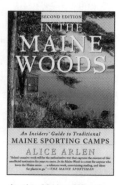
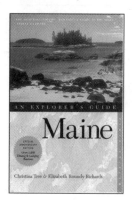